THE MASTERY OF CONSCIOUSNESS

"A most useful introduction to the teachings of Meher Baba. By carefully balancing respect for his teacher's formulations with consideration for the reader who is unfamiliar with applied mysticism, Allan Cohen has produced a book that will be of real service to anyone seeking to make a choice from among the many 'new religions.'"

—JACOB NEEDLEMAN,
author of *The New Religions*

"I feel very passionately about this book; I feel it is for young, screwed-up people, and some not-so-young or screwed-up seekers. I feel the book does everything it set out to do, it helps clear up what to Do about the spiritual path as set out by Baba. It has been needed a long time and is finally here...." —PETER TOWNSHEND,
composer, musician, The Who

Photograph by Rano Gayley. Reproduced by permission of Lawrence Reiter (Hermes).

MEHER BABA, 1964

I give you all my blessing that the spark of my divine love may implant in your hearts the deep longing for the love of God.

THE MASTERY OF CONSCIOUSNESS

An Introduction and Guide to Practical Mysticism and Methods of Spiritual Development

as given by

MEHER BABA

Compiled and Edited by

Allan Y. Cohen

HARPER COLOPHON BOOKS
Harper & Row, Publishers
New York, Hagerstown, San Francisco, London

the text of this book is printed on 100% recycled paper

 For information address Harper & Row, Publishers, Inc., 10 East 53rd Street, New York, N.Y. 10022. Published simultaneously in Canada by Fitzhenry & Whiteside Limited, Toronto.

First edition: HARPER COLOPHON BOOKS, 1977

LIBRARY OF CONGRESS CATALOG CARD NUMBER: 76-55500

ISBN: 0-06-090371-6

78 79 80 10 9 8 7 6 5 4 3 2

There is nothing irrational in true mysticism, when it is, as it should be, a vision of Reality. It is a form of perception which is absolutely unclouded; it is so practical that it can be lived every moment of life and expressed in every-day duties; and its connection with experience is so deep that, in one sense, it is the final understanding of all experience.

—MEHER BABA, *Discourses*

Contents

PART IV REFLECTIONS ON THE WAY

APPENDICES

Preface

The idea for this book germinated in 1966, a few months before I received a Harvard Ph.D. in clinical psychology. As a graduate student, my extracurricular activities included three years of experimentation with mind-altering drugs. These were in the early days of the psychedelic movement, when adventurers of inner space were trying to explore the chemical frontiers of consciousness. In August 1964 I became interested in Meher Baba through some of his followers. I was especially impressed by the exquisite profundity of his writings on the nature of consciousness. In October of that year, I received a letter written at Meher Baba's direction that overthrew my pet notions about the spiritual promise of LSD and similar drugs. As months passed I realized the accuracy of Baba's diagnosis of the illusory and temporary quality of the chemical experience.

As my "divine itch" pushed me further away from drugs, I dabbled in several kinds of esoteric writings and disciplines. I never seriously doubted that Meher Baba was one of the great spiritual masters of our time, even the Master among masters. The more I learned about Baba, the more I saw his wisdom as breathtakingly complete and his personal life as an example of flawless existence and love. But I also felt that I was a rank beginner on the spiritual path and did not deserve to become a disciple of Meher Baba until I was more spiritually advanced. Further, I did not exactly understand how Baba's path was practical for seekers who were not with him in India. I failed to realize that *anyone* can approach Baba inwardly and that he offers a practical and viable method for *any* stage of spiritual development, even for rank beginners.

This realization finally hit home during the Christmas holidays of 1965, when I visited San Francisco and spoke with Mrs. Ivy O. Duce and Mr. Don Stevens, long-time followers of Meher Baba.

Soon after heading back to Boston, I decided to give Baba's method my full energies. With a more single-minded focus on Baba, a few months later I visited the Meher Spiritual Center in Myrtle Beach, South Carolina. One April day I was talking to Miss Kitty Davy, a wonderfully experienced and dedicated disciple of Baba's. I told her of an idea for a book, intended especially for practical-minded spiritual seekers. It seemed to me that a volume was needed that zeroed in on Baba's *method*, on questions such as What does Baba actually say to *do*? Specifically, What techniques does one employ to follow Baba's path?

Miss Davy encouraged me to write up the idea and send it along to Adi K. Irani, Meher Baba's disciple-secretary. With surprise and much delight, I received a cable from India on April 25, 1966:

> **YOUR LETTER APRIL NINETEEN TO ADI MADE ME HAPPY. I APPROVE YOUR WRITING THE BOOK. MY LOVE TO YOU.**
>
> **MEHER BABA**

A letter came from Adi Irani the same week. He verified the cable, adding, "Beloved Baba wishes me to write to you that he was glad to hear of your plan to write a book about and on him, as an answer to the comments of persons introduced to him for the first time, and on general heads as outlined in your letter." The same envelope contained instructions from Baba that I and others should direct our attention to combatting the growing abuse of drugs through articles and talks. Baba especially wanted drug users to realize the spiritual alternatives to drugs. Because an instruction from a Master takes precedence over one's own request approved, this book took second priority.

I did the basic research at the Meher Center during the summer of 1966, but soon after I was compelled to take a full-time job at the University of California in Berkeley. The book was completed in snatches of free time from 1966 to mid-1976. Knowing other instances of Meher Baba's kindnesses, I have often thought that Baba's encouragement to write it had less to do with the need for such a book than with my need to focus on his words. I never met Meher Baba in the ordinary sense. In 1967 he dictated a letter requesting me not to come to India until he "called." After he died, or "dropped his body," in January 1969, I was unexpectedly, suddenly, and mysteriously drawn to India and saw Baba's body before the burial on February 7.

The final manuscript was not personally reviewed by Baba, but a preliminary draft was submitted to Adi K. Irani in the spring of 1972. A few months later and again in 1975, I flew to India and tape-recorded interviews with Baba's disciples for addition to this book. Part of an early draft was checked also by Murshida Ivy O. Duce, who was approved by Baba as primary editor of four of his books, *God Speaks, Discourses, Beams,* and *Life at Its Best.*

When the manuscript was accepted for publication, I requested attorney Ira Deitrick to create the Meher Baba Book Trust, with its own bank account to receive advances and royalties from the sale of the book. The Trust will distribute any income to three charitable organizations that Meher Baba set in motion—the Avatar Meher Baba Trust in Ahmednagar, India; the Meher Spiritual Center of Myrtle Beach, South Carolina; and Sufism Reoriented, Inc. of Walnut Creek, California.

I wish to thank the following persons and organizations for permission to reprint excerpts from various publications: Jean Adriel (*Avatar*); Francis Brabazon (*Stay with God, Journey with God);* Filis Frederick (*The Awakener);* Adi K. Irani, Sr., Meher Baba's words in *Divya Vani, The Answer, Meher Baba Journal, Meher Baba on Love, The Wisdom of Meher Baba, Sobs and Throbs, The Meher Message, The Meher Gazette, An Introductory Life Sketch, What Does Speaking the Word Mean?, At the Feet of the Master, Six Messages, In Lap of Love,* and *The Wayfarers;* Meher Baba Information, Inc. (*Darshan Hours*); Meher House Publications (*The Everything and the Nothing*); Meher Spiritual Center, Inc. (*The God-Man*); Sufism Reoriented, Inc. (*God Speaks; Discourses; Beams; Life at Its Best; Listen, Humanity; Sufism; God in a Pill?*); Universal Spiritual League of America, Inc. (*The Family Letters*); and Universal Spiritual League of Great Britain (*Sparks*).

I extend further thanks to K. S. Sarosh Irani, Nariman and Arnavaz Dadachanji, Meherjee Karkaria, Manija Irani, Eruch Jessawala, Ali Akbar Shapurzaman, Rano Gayley, Adi K. Irani, Sr., Bhau Kulchuri, Mansari Desai, and Bal Natu for their cooperation in allowing me to tape-record interviews with them.

I wish also to express my special appreciation to all those who assisted in the preparation of this volume: to Miss Kitty Davy for her original encouragement and sustaining enthusiasm; to Meher Baba's Indian circle of disciples, for their loving assistance; to editor Elisabeth Jakab for patience worthy of a saint; to H. A. Welshons for his selfless contribution; to Ira Deitrick for his donated services; to Sharon Childs for her faithful help; and to those unnamed but cherished helpers who typed, read, criticized, edited, or checked parts of the manuscript. I especially give thanks to Murshida Ivy O. Duce for her profound and compassionate guidance; to my parents for their constant affection; and to all my brothers and sisters in the pursuit of God who have, by their example, sharpened my perception of the practicalities of the spiritual path.

This book is dedicated to the One in the many.

ALLAN Y. COHEN

Introduction: A Letter to the Reader

Dear Reader,

In talking of illusion and reality, a disciple of Meher Baba once mused that the sun never really sets; it is the earth that moves. Night and clouds do not diminish the reality of the sun, only our ability to see it. From the mystic point of view, it is the same with life. If only our vision were not fogged by ignorance, we might experience the reality of true awareness.

Many individuals in the Western world have become intensely interested in altered states of consciousness and the study of inner space. New psychologies posit a natural instinct toward inner growth and higher awareness. The goal of such a drive has been called many things—love, nirvana, self-actualization, consciousness expansion, mystic vision, satori, enlightenment, and so on. A number of social scientists argue that the burgeoning interest in the intangible and the mystical derives from unstable social conditions. Others observe the vacuum of values in advanced technological civilization. They hypothesize that youth find hollow the promises of materialism and that the late 1960s and 1970s sees them searching for something more immediate and subjectively meaningful, even if "irrational." But whatever the most plausible sociological explanation, there seems to me a reality behind the quest for greater experience of truth.

I suspect that people reading these pages are special. Perhaps they perceive that there is more to life than the customs, values, and strivings that dominate contemporary society. My guess is that there is an instinct in them that sometimes whispers and sometimes cries out in many languages and forms the challenge to find real meaning in life, to become truly happy and fully conscious of who they are. For some readers the search has been unconscious or has been perceived as intellectual curiosity. Perhaps others have undergone psychotherapy or sensed deep interpersonal relationships as promising full satisfaction. Others have experimented with drugs, immersed themselves in the arts, explored Eastern philosophy, or tried meditation of some sort.

I know that certain readers feel reasonably content with life and are not desperately searching for more profound layers of consciousness; for them, I hope this volume stimulates and provokes curiosity. Other readers may have committed themselves to an inner quest; for them, I hope the book offers useful guidelines. Still other readers are already familiar with the writings of Meher Baba, many counting themselves among his followers; for them, I can only hope that the following pages refresh and enliven their love.

Editorial Philosophy

My self-imposed task as editor is to extract the essence of Meher Baba's method from thousands of pages written by, for, and about him, to enable a reader to understand Baba's approach to the mastery of consciousness, and, if he wishes, to *practice* it. Although I selected many passages reflecting the theoretical underpinnings of Baba's advised techniques, theory is presented only to fortify the logic of practice, to show *why* particular methods might be effective for a sincere seeker. In other words, this book is intended as a practical guide, not a scholarly summary or a comparative work. It concentrates on the *what* and the *how* of spiritual development according to Meher Baba.

The book does not try to evaluate Meher Baba's approach or attempt to convince readers of anything. I have proceeded on the assumption that Meher Baba is who he claims to be and knows what he is talking about. But I have also kept in mind a typical reader—intelligent, somewhat unfamiliar with applied mysticism, open-minded, one who is sufficiently skeptical to demand that any technique for producing greater awareness must be both credible and testable. The following pages contain some blazingly controversial material. I fully expect certain readers to think it heresy or to write off Meher Baba as a lunatic, huckster, or agent of Satan. However, I planned this volume fully respecting the reader's personal intuition about the relevance of Meher Baba's method. Meher Baba's way is not the only way. But many will recognize it as a way that resonates with the experience of numberless souls who have consciously undertaken the inner journey.

Textual Notes

The heart of the book is a collection of excerpts from the dictated writings of Meher Baba and transcriptions of his communications to various individuals. Meher Baba did not write any of the included passages by his own hand. Moreover, he did not speak a single word from the start of his physical silence in 1925. Until 1954, he communicated with a wooden alphabet board, pointing rapidly at individual letters that were read off by practiced disciples. After 1954, Baba gave up the use of the board and communicated through unique hand gestures, which were quickly and easily interpreted by his mandali.*

Thus, all of Meher Baba's "writings" found here have been "dictated" in one way or another and transcribed by disciples. Baba used English as his major language and dictated all his important published books in English. Occasionally, when his Eastern followers gathered, he would request that his discourses be translated into different languages. But as far as I know, almost all the excerpts in the following pages were given originally in English.

Often, Baba gave transcribers considerable latitude in the verbal expression of his communications. Most often, Baba did not give word-for-word dictation, and he reviewed manuscripts only for his major works. Thus, each transcriber had his linguistic idiosyncrasies, which are reflected in grammatical and stylistic differences apparent in the excerpts. If literary awkwardness appears, it is probably due to the transcriber, since Baba himself was a masterful writer and poet. However, even though some of Baba's recorded words and phrasing are not necessarily *just* as he would have written them, they are a reasonably accurate rendering of his messages.

*The "mandali" are the members of a circle of Baba's closest disciples. The term usually refers to those men and women disciples who lived with or near to Baba and who were totally under his personal direction.

Especially for his major texts, which he personally approved or revised, it is safe to say that misconstrual of Baba's hand gestures or variation in transcription is not a significant source of error.

For the sake of accuracy, I have kept all the punctuation, spelling, and capitalization of the original sources, even though doing so produces glaring and bothersome inconsistencies. I have made only rare exceptions to this policy, including the deletion of excessive italics (particularly from the *Discourses*). In addition, I sometimes substituted brackets for the original parentheses when I had good reason to believe that a word or phrase had been inserted by a previous editor. I also made a very few changes in punctuation, but only when it seemed absolutely necessary and when I was convinced that Baba had not reviewed the transcription in question. Whether they appear in Baba's excerpts or in my editorial commentary, Indian or unfamiliar terms and phrases are defined in the Glossary (Appendix B).

I have followed the convention of using the masculine in referring to the seeker, aspirant, or disciple as "he" or "him." However, Baba makes no spiritual distinction between the capabilities of male and female seekers. Similarly, reference to God as "He" or "Him" is never meant to imply gender. Meher Baba assigns no separate sexual identity to God.

Whatever the variations in transcription and language, readers may be sure they are seeing the essence of Meher Baba's "teachings." Baba had no special "secrets" given to some but unavailable for others; he freely gave the core secrets of the universe and the spiritual path. Baba did not require one to be a special initiate to receive wisdom. However, there are many layers of depth and meaning in his messages, and he would adapt his communications to particular audiences. For example, many passages are taken from Baba's discourses to his very closest disciples in intimate settings. They may appear to set unreasonably high standards for a seeker who is just beginning. Actually, the general principles are applicable for all, but Baba tuned them to the level and readiness of his listeners. Baba never compromised the truth, nor was he reluctant to stress those spiritual orientations that most efficiently catapult the seeker to the ultimate goal. At the same time, Baba often said that a Master never asks for the impossible, and expects different levels of effort and results from persons at different stages of the spiritual journey.

Overview and Apologies

The book consists of four separate parts; each part includes several chapters and is introduced by a continuation of this Letter to the reader. Part I ("Preparation") presents the highlights of Meher Baba's life and his ideas about the search for higher consciousness. Part II ("General Methods") surveys the general ways to the mastery of consciousness as well as the pitfalls of incomplete or fraudulent methods. Part III ("Specific Techniques"), the heart of the book, outlines the essence of Meher Baba's method, including the way of the Master, Meher Baba as Avatar and guide, and the ways of following Baba. Part IV ("Reflections on the Way") is intended to clarify issues such as Baba's spiritual claims, problems of following him after he left his physical body, and speculation on the future of the Meher Baba movement. The Appendices provide assistance to readers wishing to follow up their interest in Baba's approach.

I realize that this collection is not nearly complete. Although there is some comfort in knowing that the full picture is contained in the totality of Baba's publications, I have taken the risk of fragmenting the organic nature of his writings. If one cuts out small sections of a complexly woven blanket, there is always the danger of obscuring the beauty of the overall pattern.

I have another concern. In trying to present a coherent and logical flow to the book, my style may suffer from too much intellectualization. Of course, both readers and I must be patient with the incongruity of describing nonverbal experience in words and categories. But my editorial comments underrepresent the quality of heart involved in Baba's method. A parallel, less verbal essence of his approach is found in the thousands of touching human accounts of Baba's love, compassion, wisdom, and gentle humor. I could include only a few such stories here. Meher Baba's path is comprehensible to thought and intelligence, but it cannot be applied by the mind alone.

I fully realize a more significant risk—the interjection of editorial commentary. From the beginning, I wished to keep my own comments to a minimum, hoping to reduce the risks of interpretation, but I find I have contributed more to the text than I had planned.

Every extra interpretive word carries with it a measure of anxiety on my part—a fear of tarnishing that which is pure, a dread of distorting that which is perfect. Judging from centuries past, there is the tragic possibility that a Master's words will be misinterpreted, even altered, and the distortions crystallized after he leaves his physical body. In this book, all the direct statements of Baba are set in boldface type. Ultimately, all other material is expendable. My editorial or interpretive comments are no more than reasoned speculation. I claim no special spiritual authority or state of consciousness beyond that of a struggling beginner on the path. Even though Meher Baba approved the writing of this book, he did not personally review the final manuscript, so that any editorial cement is fallible. I emphasize my limitations not out of self-deprecation or excessive humility. I do so out of a sensitivity to misinterpretations of the message of the God-Man and from a personal hope that my editorial involvement will not add confusion to the love and truth expressed by Meher Baba.

PART I

Preparation

Introduction

Dear Reader,

Part I begins our shared exploration of the way of Meher Baba. Hopefully, these first two chapters will serve as a preparation for understanding the chapters on methods that follow.

Chapter 1 presents a historical sketch of Meher Baba's life, focusing on him as both man and Master. In Chapter 2, I have selected excerpts reflecting Baba's metaphysical overview. "Method" implies a procedure directed at a goal, and Baba explains the goal of consciousness, the real motive underlying the human spirit. He also discusses other basic issues in the study of spiritual motivation. Thus, Part I introduces the *what* and the *why* as a foundation for the *how,* which is explained in Parts II and III.

CHAPTER 1

The Life of Meher Baba: Man and Master

To penetrate into the essence of all being and significance, and to release the fragrance of that inner attainment for the guidance and benefit of others, by expressing, in the world of forms, truth, love, purity and beauty—this is the sole game which has any intrinsic and absolute worth. All other happenings, incidents and attainments in themselves can have no lasting importance.

—MEHER BABA, *Discourses*

Fortunately, the details of Meher Baba's life are very well documented by written records, by witnesses still living, and by Baba's own recollections. Given the richness of verifiable material, a full biography could fill thousands of pages. Here I have attempted only to present the high points of Baba's external activities from his physical birth to his physical death. The implications of his unusual experiences and methods of working will be discussed later on.

The Childhood and Adolescence of Merwan Irani

Meher Baba was born as Merwan Sheriar Irani on February 25, 1894, in Poona, India. His parents were Persians of the Zoroastrian faith who migrated to India. His father, Sheriar M. Irani, had dedicated his young life to seeking God as a spiritual wayfarer. However, he experienced an inner voice that commanded him to give up his asceticism, marry, and have children. The voice declared that one of his children would be a great spiritual leader. Shortly after, he married, and in time his wife, Shirinmai, gave birth to eight children.

Merwan, the second child, was a healthy and happy boy, a bit mischievous but gentle and unselfish. Baba reminisced about his childhood: **When I was a boy I did not know anything. I had nothing to do with spirituality. My father, who was a *dervish*, had roamed throughout Persia and India, begging and contemplating God. He taught me some verses from Hafiz and other poets, but I had no interest in this. I preferred games and I found myself the leader of others.**[1]

As a teen-ager Merwan's personal interests broadened. He did very well in schoolwork, excelled at cricket and field hockey, became a class leader, and was well liked by both classmates and teachers in his Roman Catholic school, perhaps the finest school in Poona. He began to enjoy Western and Eastern literature, from Shakespeare and Wordsworth to the great Persian mystic poet Hafiz. He wrote poems in different Indian dialects, in Persian, and in English, many of which were published in newspapers and journals. At fifteen he was a great fan of mystery fiction and wrote a story that was published nationally. Merwan graduated from St. Vincent's High School with honors and went on to Poona's Deccan College at the age of seventeen. The beginning of his college career demonstrated the same academic success and acceptance as a natural leader trusted by his classmates.

But Merwan Irani was never to finish college. Up through his eighteenth year his life, though laudable, was hardly extraordinary. Soon after, on a hot day in 1913, his normal existence came to an abrupt end.

The Unveiling

The unprecedented set of events that happened to this Deccan College sophomore defies traditional scientific explanation. Initially, it centered on an astounding woman almost 107 years old named Hazrat Babajan. She could always be found under a certain tree in the center of Poona and was revered as one of the great saints and

Masters of the time. Tens of thousands came to visit this universal guru, to hear a few discourses and sit in her highly charged presence.

Merwan passed by Babajan on his bicycle route home along the dusty roads. While still attending classes, he spent more and more time with this remarkable woman: **I was drawn to her as steel to a magnet.**[2] One day in May 1913, Babajan kissed Merwan on the forehead, symbolizing some simultaneous inner charge: **With just a kiss on the forehead, between the eyebrows, Babajan made me experience . . . thrills of indescribable bliss which continued for about nine months.**[3] Experiencing continual jolts of spiritual ecstasy, Merwan spent time each night at Babajan's feet. One evening, when she was in a talkative mood, he stayed longer than usual. It is reported that she pointed her finger at him, declaring, "This child of mine will create a great sensation in the world and do immense good to humanity."[4] She looked at him intently, and he made his way home. Soon after, he experienced an indescribable and total state of consciousness, which blasted away any awareness of the ordinary world. Decades later, Baba explained that during the night, Babajan made him **realize in a flash the infinite bliss of self-realization** [God-realization].[5]

The unveiling of realization had some powerful side effects. Merwan's mother discovered him lying in bed, absolutely oblivious to ordinary consciousness. She thought him seriously ill. He remained immobile for three days, after which he began to move around like an automaton. Baba talked about these events some forty years later: **. . . for nine months, God knows, I was in that state to which very, very few go. I had no consciousness of my body, or of anything else. I roamed about taking no food. My mother thought I was mad, and called the doctor. My father understood, but said nothing. The doctors could not do anything. I did not sleep. . . .**[6]

My sleepless, staring, vacant eyes worried my mother most. She believed and told others that I had gone mad. In her anguish she could not refrain from going once to Babajan and demanding to know what she had done to me. . . . Babajan indicated to my mother that I was intended to shake the world into wakefulness, but that meant nothing to Shirinmai in her distress.[7]

Certainly, we can understand her distress. Merwan neither slept nor ate for nine full months. Complete medical treatment was initiated, including shots of morphine to induce sleep, but with no effect. Then suddenly, one day in 1914, another phase began: **From that moment, instead of the Divine Bliss that I was in, for nine months I was in such tortures that no one in the world can understand. I used to bang my head to relieve my pain. I scarred my head on floors and walls. I could not contain myself. It was as if the whole universe was on my head.**[8]

He was sent to live with his brother in Bombay and became somewhat more comfortable in the ordinary world. **Later on** [April 1915] **I also began to go for long distances on foot or by vehicle. . . . Finally** [December 1915], **I felt impelled to call on Sai Baba, the Perfect Master among Masters.* . . . Despite the crowds I intuitively prostrated myself before him on the road. When I arose, Sai Baba looked straight at me and exclaimed, "*Parvardigar*"** [God-Almighty-Sustainer].

I then felt drawn to walk to the nearby temple of Khandoba in which Maharaj [Shri Upasni Maharaj] **was staying in seclusion. He had been living under Sai Baba's direct guidance for over three years. . . . When I came near enough to him, Maharaj greeted me, so to speak, with a stone which he threw at me with great force. It struck me on my forehead exactly where Babajan had kissed me, hitting with such force that it drew blood. The mark of that injury is still on my forehead. But that blow from Maharaj was the stroke of *dnyan* (divine knowledge).**[9]

Merwan then spent several years in the company of those still-revered Masters and was given their close attention. He became more and more normally conscious of the ordinary world, while simultaneously experiencing the bliss of realization and the intense suffering connected with the consciousness of the world of illusion (see Chapter 2). The final transition from Merwan Irani to Meher Baba, a fully integrated spiritual Master, came in 1921. **After becoming almost three-fourths normally conscious while retaining full superconsciousness, I went to Sakori and stayed for six months** [July–December 1921] **near Maharaj. At the end of this period Maharaj made me *know* fully what I am, just as Babajan had made me *feel* in a flash what I am. During those six months Maharaj and**

*There are five Perfect Masters, fully realized beings who operate the spiritual hierarchy. See Chapter 7.

I used to sit near each other in a hut behind closed doors almost every night. On one such occasion Maharaj folded his hands to me and said, "Merwan, you are the Avatar and I salute you."[10]

The Young Spiritual Master

Thus, at twenty-eight Merwan S. Irani began to function as an independent spiritual master. **For about four months after this** [January–May 1922] **I stayed in a small *jhopdi*** [thatched hut]. **It was built for me temporarily on the edge of some fields in the very thinly populated area of . . . Poona. In this manner I began to live independently, surrounded by men who formed the nucleus of the *mandali*. One of these was the first to start addressing me as "Baba."** [Literally, "Meher Baba" means "Compassionate Father."]

Some of the men were drawn intuitively to me long before they had any clear idea of my inner state. Others were attracted to me by hints from Babajan and Maharaj. And still others I drew directly to me. At that time both Babajan and Maharaj began telling various people, referring to me, that "The child is now capable of moving the whole world at a sign from his finger." Once [May 1922] **Maharaj addressed a large gathering of the *mandali* and said, "Listen to me most carefully. I have handed over my key** [spiritual charge] **now to Merwan, and henceforth you are all to stick to him and do as he instructs you." . . . Still others, Maharaj asked individually to follow me.**[11]

In 1922 Baba established his first ashram at a house in Bombay, where more than forty men of all faiths stayed with him for many months under strict spiritual guidelines. The next fairly permanent center was an old World War I military camp near the small village of Arangaon, some ninety miles north of Poona. This settlement, now the location of Baba's tomb, came to be known as Meherabad ("abad" means "flourishing"). However, until January 1925, Baba had his mandali on the move, traveling all over India, undergoing severe hardship, with Baba fasting almost all of the time in connection with some inner work.

Finally, the group settled in Meherabad. **For almost two years** [until November 1926] **it was like a small model town. In it lived about five hundred souls, working in the hospital, the dispensary and the schools. There were also *ashrams* for boys, men and**

women, and shelters for the poor and for lepers, all of which were established here in connection with my work.[12] While activities in Meherabad revolved around selfless service to the poor and infirm, Baba was putting his disciples through excruciating spiritual training.

Somewhat unobtrusively, Baba began maintaining physical silence on July 10, 1925. **Despite my silence . . . I continued all my usual activities. At that time I communicated by writing on a slate, and also for more than a year wrote for a number of hours daily on a work which remains unseen and unpublished to this day.**[13] No one is known to have read the manuscript Baba was writing. After completing the book, he had it kept under lock and key with instructions that the mandali must not look at it. Occasionally, Baba referred to it as his "Bible," implying that it contained hitherto unknown secrets, the story of his own experiences in the superconscious state, and revolutionary new information relating to science. He said that the book would be published when the time was right. As of mid-1977, the location of the manuscript remains a mystery.

In January 1927 Baba gave up writing except for his signature, "M. S. Irani." He started using an English alphabet board; his disciples became so accustomed to reading Baba's darting fingers that fluent and efficient conversations were conducted with ease. Baba discarded even the board in 1954 when he began to use hand gestures, again fluently expressed in words by disciples. In any description of Baba's life or activities since 1927, when it is reported that "Baba said . . . ," communication by the alphabet board or physical gestures is presumed.

After terminating the community functions at Meherabad, Baba set up a unique boys' school called Meher Ashram, which was open to all castes, races, and nationalities.[14] After the boys were taught English, Baba concentrated on their general welfare and spiritual upliftment. In March 1928 the boarding school was divided. The new portion, Prem ("Love") Ashram, "housed the boys most awakened to love."

The Traveling Master

The decade from 1929 to 1939 was marked by extensive travel, Baba taking his close disciples on several tours of India and ten visits to

Europe and the West. Baba's Indian "lovers" (he preferred this term to "devotees" or "followers") stayed behind in India, where Baba was active between journeys. On his travels to the West, Baba held interviews with selected Westerners interested in him and also took his disciples to places associated with spirituality, such as the residences of great saints of the past. He preferred relatively little publicity, although on occasion he granted journalistic interviews.

As usual, his work with new Western disciples was unostentatious and very human; he rarely emphasized esoteric exercises, meditation, diet, or other techniques usually associated with the popular image of Eastern masters. Yet thousands of incidents occurred in Baba's presence, incidents laden with meaning and bringing about deep inner changes in those he met. Baba's companions only rarely saw those events that seem spiritually glamorous in the public mind: "After stopping in Paris for three days and in London for six, he traveled to Zurich. He spent one of his ten days here in seclusion on a mountain-top, with his group watching from a near-by peak. Suddenly a heavy rain-storm descended upon them, drenching them to the skin. As they looked over toward the mountain where Baba sat they were amazed to see him encircled in golden light, with no sign of rain touching his person."[15]

Inside India

Meher Baba's travels during the 1940s were also extensive, but took place primarily within India. During this period Baba took extraordinary steps to contact the poor, the blind, and the infirm—especially lepers, whom he called "beautiful birds in ugly cages." He would often bathe them, bow down to their feet, and present them with small gifts. Also concerned with the mentally ill, he once supervised his disciples in the compassionate care of the emotionally disturbed at a special ashram.

But the primary objects of Baba's hunt for humanity in the 1940s were the spiritually advanced. Baba, mostly incognito, toured at least 75,000 miles within the Indian subcontinent to contact such souls. Some of them were ordinary sadhus, persons seeking the spiritual path by renouncing the worldly life. Baba's unique work, however, was with those advanced souls so in love with God, so intoxicated with experiences on higher levels of consciousness, that they do not seem bound by nature's elementary rules. In India these persons are called *masts* (pronounced "musts") and, despite their eccentricities, are greatly revered by spiritually alert Indians.

Often acting like an ordinary lunatic, the inner madness of the *mast* is a spiritual one: **The mind of an ordinary madman has failed to adapt itself to the problems of the material world, and has fled permanently into the realm of make-believe to escape an intolerable material situation. But a God-mad man, though he has lost the balance of his mind and the insight into his abnormal state, has not come to this condition by failing to solve his worldly troubles, but has lost his sanity through continually thinking about God.[16] *Masts* are those who become permanently unconscious in part or whole of their physical bodies, actions and surroundings, due to their absorption in their intense love and longing for God.[17]**

Although Baba's outward meetings with the *masts* were unspectacular, he gave some hint of their inner significance: **The *masts* alone know how they love me and I alone know how I love them. I work for the *masts*, and knowingly or unknowingly they work for me.[18]** On other occasions Baba explained that he assisted the *masts* with their spiritual work elsewhere in the world.

The immense physical difficulties of his journeys never reduced Baba's compassion for those who suffered. Even though he traveled incognito, word would spread through villages that the Master would not refuse to see anyone who was sick, destitute, or despairing, and countless individuals came to Baba for his blessing. Some of these incidents were spontaneous, like one personally witnessed by Jean Adriel:

> When we reached the top of the mountain, a poor emaciated dog came limping from the bushes toward the group. His face was almost eaten away by some disease. The only visible eye looked pathetically at us, as he whined miserably. A couple of the younger women cried out hysterically and involuntarily drew back from him. Baba instantly came forward and, leaning down, gently placed his hand upon the running sores. The dog sat down on his haunches and turned his face up to Baba, obviously grateful for the healing balm which was being poured upon him. His whine changed into a deep sigh of contentment as the hand of the God-man wiped away the intolerable pain.[19]

The period from October 1949 to February 1952 brought a new and symbolically important phase of Baba's activities, which he called "the New Life." During this period,

> Baba lived what he called his life of complete external renunciation. . . . The full story of the hardships and crises incident to this life of self-created helplessness remains known only to the companions Baba took with him in his New Life adventure. These were the handful of men and women who had chosen and were allowed to participate in the venture. They traveled with him from place to place in distant parts of India, mostly on foot, and under the most trying conditions, having no ready shelters, no money and no day-to-day provisions to draw upon.[20]

Baba told his disciples that he would become "helpless and hopeless," as should they, renouncing all but surrender to God and His help. In this period Baba played down his own role as a spiritual Master and became a "companion," although his control and direction of the group remained total.

The Last Decades

After Baba declared his intense New Life to be complete in 1952, he initiated a decade of communication with the public in both the East and West. In the spring of 1952, he made a major visit to the United States, which included activities at the spiritual center dedicated to his work in Myrtle Beach, South Carolina. During an auto trip to California weeks later, Baba's car was hit head-on by another car near Prague, Oklahoma. Baba's arm and leg were broken, yet he bore his serious injuries in perfect calm, even beaming satisfaction. Baba had predicted a personal disaster years before and afterward said, **It was necessary that it should happen in America. God willed it so.**[21] This accident and another severe one in India in 1956 that destroyed his hip joint were to saddle Baba with nagging physical pain throughout the 1950s and 1960s.

Despite the pain, Baba plunged back into work in India. During the 1950s he gave scores of mass *darshan* programs, in which thousands came to receive the physical presence and blessing ("darshan") of the Master. Most of Baba's important books and discourses were given or published during this period.* Returning to the West in 1956, Baba made his most extensive tour of the United States. He returned again in 1958 to give *sahavas* (sharing the company of a

*See Appendix C for descriptions of all major publications by and about Meher Baba.

master) at the Center in Myrtle Beach, mostly just mixing with his lovers.

In India Baba lived primarily at Meherazad, a countryside ashram not far from Meherabad and the city of Ahmednagar. He occasionally received visitors but often went into seclusion. Between 1962 and 1968, Baba withdrew more from public functions and his physical suffering increased. He stressed the great importance of his inner "universal work" at the time. A few mass darshans were held in the early sixties, but the number of visitors was gradually decreased.

In 1966 and 1967, Baba's relative seclusion intensified. He began to request the curtailment of casual mail written to him by his lovers and permitted even fewer visitors. Nevertheless, he was always acutely aware of contemporary trends around the world. In late 1965 he entered firmly into the controversy surrounding psychedelic drug use, instructing his lovers against the nonmedical use of chemicals. He also began to encourage the direct spreading of news regarding his existence and his "message of Love and Truth."

The Last Months

Whatever the nature of Baba's internal work, his health had been failing for some time, although he had occasional periods of unexplainable recovery. In September of 1968, he heralded the end of this phase of his seclusion: **My work is done. It is completed 100% to my satisfaction. The result of this work will also be 100%.**[22] Reacting to the longing of his lovers to see him, many for the first time, Baba said, **I also am impatient for them to see me. But the time has yet not come—so my lovers and I, we must wait a while longer.**[23]

Finally, on October 13, Meher Baba announced that he would break his seclusion from April 10 to June 10, 1969, and receive his lovers at a darshan. Although Baba lovers received the news with great joy, the mandali felt that Baba's body could not possibly stand the strain. As the autumn of 1968 progressed, Baba's health became worse, although he assured the mandali that all would be well. His physical symptoms were baffling to physicians called in from Bombay and Poona. Blood tests determined that any ordinary person in his condition would be in a coma and mental delirium.

But there was no interruption in alertness, and Baba joked heartily with the astounded doctors.

In late January 1969, the mandali observed further deterioration in his physical condition, reflected in intense pain, but Baba refused to go into Poona for diagnostic tests. He told them that his condition had no medical grounds at all, that it was due purely to the strain of his spiritual work. All this time he was hinting at something important that was imminent.

During the last days of January, Baba's body was shaken by great muscular spasms, causing excruciating pain. The mandali said they had never seen him suffer so, not even from the serious automobile accidents and their devastating side effects. And yet Baba never lost complete mental awareness or good humor, so the mandali were shocked when his body shook with a great spasm and ceased to function fifteen minutes after noon on January 31, 1969. According to previously given instructions, they took the body to Baba's tomb at Meherabad and placed it in an uncovered crypt, where it lay for seven days, unusually resistant to decomposition. Thousands flocked to have one last look at the Master's "cloak," and a simple burial followed around noon on February 7.

Meher Baba: The Personality

So ends a brief biography of Merwan Irani–Meher Baba. But the facts cannot convey the quality of Meher Baba's personal influence, just as one can describe the external attributes of a luscious fruit but never really communicate the flavor until it is tasted. However, from thousands of accounts, certain characteristics stand out that give a tiny glimpse of some of Baba's profoundly rich qualities.

In appearance,

> Meher Baba was of medium height, about five feet six. As a young man his build was slender, and films show him moving with a graceful, floating walk—with which he many times covered thirty miles a day, for days on end, so that his most vigorous companions could scarcely keep pace with him. Later, after his two severe car accidents, his body became thick, since almost any form of movement gave him pain; but when you put your arms round him . . . his body seemed simultaneously firm and insubstantial, as though having solidity but little weight. As a rule he wore Indian dress with sandals or else with his feet bare, and since they

> were almost never confined in shoes, his toes stood out separate and strong. His hands looked powerful enough to crack stones, but he moved his fingers with astonishing delicacy, as though playing an invisible musical instrument, to convey his silent meaning; while doing so he would often look up at his interpreter with a humorous, trustful gaze. His expression changed continually, but it was particularly through his eyes that the pattern of thought and feeling was conveyed. Intensely black, they would in a few seconds lovingly greet his audience, sparkle with laughter, or contemplate some situation with a sternness there was no resisting or escaping.[24]

Frequently mentioned by observers was Baba's naturalness, his way of putting everyone at ease, of being a friend and superb host. Even those who accepted him as God incarnate felt extremely comfortable around him. He wore no religious markings and mixed freely with everyone. Baba was physically affectionate, preferring his followers to embrace him lovingly rather than bow down to him. In films he is seen clapping backs, tweaking ears, gently grasping hands, equally natural with men, women, and children. Baba never married and led a life of complete celibacy, once commenting with a smile that for him sex did not exist.

Baba's naturalness was reflected especially in his playfulness and humor. He enjoyed playing games with his lovers, especially with children, and he was a top-notch Ping-Pong player and marble shooter. Baba cracked jokes constantly when the occasion called for lightness. He loved humorous stories and often called on certain lovers to tell jokes, sometimes just before or after powerful spiritual discourses. He enjoyed being entertained by amateur skits, songs, and dances put on by followers, some of which included loving satires on him. When one new follower expressed surprise at Baba's keen sense of humor, Baba reminded him, **Divinity includes all that is beautiful and gracious. . . . How, then, could you expect a Perfect Being to be devoid of a sense of humor?**[25]

In his daily living patterns Baba maintained a very simple, usually vegetarian diet, although the diet was not necessarily encouraged for his lovers. When he went on extended fasts, he stunned the younger mandali with his unbelievable energy and stamina. One startling fact is that Baba never slept in the ordinary sense. He often rested for about three hours each night, but as his disciples testified, he never lost consciousness. Baba once explained that unconscious sleep is not required by those who have transcended ordinary dual consciousness: **In superconsciousness the soul experiences itself as all-mighty, its bliss is unbounded and its continuous awareness of itself as the infinite truth admits no slightest interruption. . . .**[26]

When Baba kept strict seclusion, it was not for his personal benefit but for his work. Often he would come out of a few hours' seclusion more exhausted than after weeks of walking across India with no food. Baba was asked why he subjected himself to such discomfort and limitations if he was spiritually perfect. He explained that he had no need for self-denial and never fasted for the reasons yogis do. He also stated that physical confinement was only apparent, not real to him. **It does not inconvenience me, for walls do not bind me. For certain kinds of work which I have to do in non-physical realms, I prefer to shut myself up in a small place. It was for the same reason that Jesus, after attaining perfection, stayed for thirty continuous days on a mountain where he did not allow even his intimate disciples to approach him.**[27]

Baba never kept money, and he touched currency only when passing it on to the poor or the *masts:* **It is only money offered with love that I accept and disburse for my work.** He said, **Money has absolutely no connection with love, and love is the only thing of real value. No one could ever win Godhood from me in exchange for all the money in the world, but he who loves me intensely can become God without possessing or giving me a single pie** [cent].[28]

Those disciples who lived with Baba existed very simply. Baba encouraged other lovers to continue active life in the ordinary world. All of the closest disciples, after years of spiritual training and ego reduction, have the same quality of naturalness combined with selfless humility. They are all distinct personalities, quite human in their different tastes and talents; but their love, kindness, incorruptible character, and utter dedication to Baba are the exquisite commonalities.

Perhaps the best summation of Baba's activities was given by Baba himself in the 1950s: **To those who wish to know about my activities I can only say that as far as my inner life and internal activities are concerned, only God and those who are one with God can know and understand. As far as my external activities are concerned regarding my work with the God-intoxicated, saints, "sadhus" and the poor; of contacting them, working with them,** serving them and bowing down to them in devotion, they have all been recorded by a disciple of mine in *The Wayfarers*.

I enjoy games, chiefly cricket, playing marbles, flying kites and also listening to music, although I can do so only on rare occasions. From time immemorial, I have been playing with the Mayavic universe and this enjoyment of playing still persists. I sometimes see motion pictures (mostly humorous ones), and enjoy my real state of being the eternal Producer of the vast, ever-changing, never-ending film called the universe. I also find relaxation in listening to humorous stories, all the time being aware of the humor that lies in the aspect of the soul, which is the source of infinite power and glory, being made to feel so helpless in its human bondage of ignorance arising from its various forms of duality. . . .

I do not interfere with any religion and permit all to follow unhindered their own creeds. When compared with love for God, external ceremonials have no value. . . .

From the beginningless beginning to the present day I Am What I Am, irrespective of praise or universal opposition, and will remain so to the endless end.[29]

CHAPTER 2

The Quest of Consciousness

It is not so much that you are within the cosmos as that the cosmos is within you.

—MEHER BABA, *Life at Its Best*

Certain events in Meher Baba's life raise obvious questions that are explored later in this book. For now, it might be most helpful to examine Baba's ideas about the need for methods of spiritual development. Methods make no sense without goals, goals imply values, and the existence of values implies motivation.

To Meher Baba, the real desire of human beings consists in the "quest," that urge of consciousness to grow in wisdom and experience through many life forms. This most basic drive operates unconsciously for most, consciously for the occasional seeker. Baba sees the quest and its goal in at least two facets—the human and the cosmic.

Seeds of the Search

Meher Baba comments on the human experience of the quest, man's **longing for happiness and searching desperately for some means of breaking out of the trap which his life has become. It is not his fault if he assumes that the solution to his deep dissatisfaction lies in a sensual life, or in achievement in business or the social world, or in a life of exciting experiences. Neither is it his fault if life is not usually long enough to teach him factually that he would find even more profound disillusionment if these goals were to be fulfilled to the hilt.[1]**

God either exists or does not exist. If He exists, search for Him is

amply justified. And if He does not exist, there is nothing to lose by seeking Him. But man does not usually turn to a real search for God as a matter of voluntary and joyous enterprise. He has to be driven to this search by disillusionment with those worldly things which allure him and from which he cannot deflect his mind. . . . He tries as best he can to have pleasures of the senses and to avoid different kinds of suffering. . . . While he thus goes through the daily round of varied experiences, there often arises some occasion when he begins to ask himself, "*What is the end of all this?*" . . . He can no longer be content with the fleeting things of this life and he is thoroughly skeptical about the ordinary values which he had so far accepted without doubt. . . . In the moment of such *divine desperateness* a man makes the important decision to discover and realise the aim of life. There thus comes into existence a true search for lasting values.[2]

In Baba's view, the masking effect of limited experience is a necessary contrast for the appreciation of perfect consciousness. **One has to experience being caged if one is to appreciate freedom. If in the entire span of its life the fish has not come out of the water even once, it has no chance of appreciating the value of water. . . . In the same way, if life had been constantly free and manifested no bondage man would have missed the real significance of freedom. To experience spiritual bondage and know intense desire to be free from it are both a preparation for the full enjoyment of the freedom which is to come.**

As the fish which is taken out of water longs to go back in the water, the aspirant who has perceived the goal longs to be united with God. In fact, the longing to go back to the source is present in *each* being from the very time that it is separated from the source by the veil of ignorance. . . .[3]

Even as the individual can be wrong in his convictions regarding his own nature, so he is often quite wrong about the nature of the world around him. In reality, it is a world of illusion that separates him from his true birthright of freedom and happiness in oneness with the One. . . . If this illusion can be shattered, the shackles which bind happiness are automatically shattered as well. But how to shatter the illusion?[4]

The first step for anyone, Baba hints, is to act on that divine itch in moments of existential desperation, to break up old life patterns and plunge into the drama of Self-discovery. The true hero of this cosmic drama is God disguised as every individual soul, striving to comprehend its real nature.

The Journey of the Soul to the Oversoul

For many spiritual teachers and aspirants, it is enough to presume the existence of the inherent drive of consciousness to perfect itself. The *why* of it all remains a mystery. But Meher Baba lays it all out. Although he points out that intellectual knowledge of metaphysics guarantees no particular inner advancement, his explanation of the creation, purpose, and evolution of the universe may be the most explicit and comprehensive ever written.[5]

Meher Baba's metaphysics depends upon only one basic assumption and its corollary: infinite existence exists, and it is capable of consciousness. In elaborate detail he explains how the universe is an arena where infinite existence, identifying with the apparently limited soul, becomes more and more conscious of its oneness with itself as the Oversoul. Thus, **The sole purpose of creation is that the soul should be able to enjoy the infinite state of the Oversoul consciously. Although the soul eternally exists in and with the Oversoul in an inviolable unity, it cannot be conscious of this unity independently of the creation, which is within the limitations of time. It must therefore evolve consciousness before it can realise its true status and nature as being identical with the Infinite Oversoul, which is *One without a second.***[6] For Baba, "God" is infinite existence—simultaneously infinitely aware when identifying with creation and semiconscious when identifying with the apparently limited soul.

The implications of Baba's metaphysics are literally mind-boggling, but Baba uses a helpful analogy to our own ordinary states of consciousness: unconscious sleep, the dream state, and the awake state. When we sleep deeply, we have no idea who we really are, yet we have an inherent urge to wake up. Because of our very nature, sooner or later we move toward full consciousness, most often through the dream state. While dreaming, we are quite thoroughly convinced of a false and limiting identity; we are quite sure that we are a character in the dream and that the dream environment is fully real, replete with physical, emotional, and mental experience. If another dream character told us we were dreaming, that everything we perceived was not separate but truly one, that we had semiconsciously created the whole experienced world, we might think them out of touch with reality. But we realize the truth of it when we awake in the morning and remember the dream.

According to Meher Baba, a similar condition extends to a higher sphere of consciousness, one which experiences ordinary waking life as an advanced dream: **Here you are all sitting in this hall thinking that your being here is real—but I assure you, you are only dreaming it. Say, tonight, when you go to sleep, you are dreaming that you are sitting here, and someone comes in your dream and tells you you are only dreaming. You will reply, "I am not dreaming, I am actually experiencing sitting here listening to Baba's discourse with all the others around me!" But in the morning you will awake and remember it as a dream. So I tell you that one day you will really awaken and know for certain that everything you have done was only a dreaming. I am the Ancient One—so is each one of you. But whereas I have awakened, you are still held in your dreams.**[7] Waking from the dream of separateness and self-imposed limitation *is* the mystic path.

The Journey Summarized

In his discourses, Meher Baba has explained fully how the individualized soul gets caught up in the dream of illusion, why it starts with very finite consciousness, and how it goes through a systematic evolution. Essentially, consciousness identifies with various impressions *(sanskaras)*, experiencing the world through more and more complex physical forms, eventually reaching the human form. The soul then reincarnates systematically to gain necessary experience. Finally, it begins to shed false impressions and false identity in order to tread the inner path toward full Self-realization.

In the beginning, because it had not evolved consciousness, the soul was unconscious of its identity with the Oversoul, and hence, though part and parcel of the Oversoul, it could not realise its own identity with it or experience infinite peace, bliss, power and knowledge. Even after the evolution of consciousness it could not realise the state of the Oversoul (although it is all the time in and with the Oversoul) because its consciousness is confined to the

phenomenal world owing to the *sanskaras* connected with the evolution of consciousness. Even on the Path, the soul is not conscious of itself, but is conscious only of the gross, subtle and mental worlds which are its own illusory shadows. At the end of the Path, however, the soul frees itself from all *sanskaras* and desires connected with the gross, subtle and mental worlds; and it becomes possible for it to free itself from the illusion of being finite, which came into existence owing to its identification with the gross, subtle and mental bodies. At this stage the soul completely transcends the phenomenal world and becomes *Self-conscious* and *Self-realised*. For attaining this goal, the soul must retain its full consciousness and at the same time know itself to be different from the *Sharira* (gross body), *Prana* (subtle body, which is the vehicle of desires and vital forces) and *Manas* (mental body, which is the seat of the mind), and also as being beyond the gross, subtle and mental worlds.

The soul has to emancipate itself gradually from the illusion of being finite by (1) liberating itself from the bondage of *sanskaras*, and (2) knowing itself to be different from its bodies—gross, subtle and mental. It thus annihilates the false ego (i.e., the illusion that "I am the gross body, I am the subtle body or I am the mental body"). While the soul thus frees itself from its illusion, it still retains full consciousness, which now results in Self-knowledge and realisation of the Truth. Escaping through the cosmic illusion and realising with full consciousness its identity with the Infinite Oversoul, is the goal of the long journey of the soul.[8]

Understanding the Journey

For Meher Baba all life, whether highly conscious or not, is moving toward one ultimate goal, an adventure seeking an eternal answer to the question of existence: **There is only one question. And once you know the answer to that question there are no more to ask. . . . Out of the depths of unbroken Infinity arose the Question, Who am I? and to that Question there is only one Answer—I am God!**[9] The problem is that people do not know who they really are: **You are infinite. You are really everywhere; but you think you are the body, and therefore consider yourself limited. If you look within and**

experience your own soul in its true nature, you will realize that you are infinite and beyond all creation.[10]

The notion of God as one's real Self is the very foundation of true spirituality and mysticism. It can be found in the teachings of the greatest spiritual Masters of history and is consistent with the essence of all world religion. It seems mysterious because of the paradox that God has to be, not *reached,* only *discovered:* **The spiritual journey does not consist in gaining what a person does not have, but in the dissipation of ignorance concerning himself and life, and the growth of understanding which begins with spiritual awakening. To find God is to come to one's own self.**[11]

According to Baba, the task of realization is immense, since it **boils down to the fact that the *Atma* [soul] has to go through one hell of a thing, one after the other, in order to become Self-conscious. To become Self-conscious is to experience the "I-Am-God" State consciously.**[12] But the gargantuan difficulties of the journey are overshadowed by its ultimate reward, where **The shackles of limited individuality are broken; the world of shadows is at an end; the curtain of illusion is forever drawn. The feverishness and the agonizing distress of the pursuits of limited consciousness are replaced by the tranquility and bliss of Truth-consciousness. The restlessness and fury of temporal existence are swallowed up in the peace and stillness of Eternity.**[13] Thus, as sketched by Meher Baba, the universe is a cosmic and just playground where infinite existence, or God, in the form of innumerable souls, evolves from ignorance to full awareness, from suffering to bliss.

Orientation for the Seeker

Even though Meher Baba's explanation of the nature of reality is focused on the ultimate, his message and method is aimed at the ordinary seeker. True, the path illuminated by Meher Baba is unquestionably a mystic path. Yet his orientation is neither irrational nor impractical.

Spiritual experience involves more than can be grasped by mere intellect. This is often emphasized by calling it a mystical experience. Mysticism is often regarded as something anti-intellectual, obscure and confused, or impractical and unconnected with experience. In fact, true mysticism is none of these. There is

nothing irrational in true mysticism when it is, as it should be, a vision of Reality. It is a form of perception which is absolutely unclouded, and so practical that it can be lived every moment of life and expressed in everyday duties. Its connection with experience is so deep that, in one sense, it is the final understanding of all experience. . . . Real spiritual experience involves not only realisation of the soul on higher planes, but also a right attitude towards worldly duties. If it loses its connection with the different phases of life, what we have is a neurotic reaction that is far from being a spiritual experience.[14]

A seeker may rightfully demand *personal* experience of the emerging truth, but **he is conscious of the limitations of his own individual experience and refrains from making it the measure of all possibilities. He has an open mind towards all things which are beyond the scope of his experience.**[15]

The serious seeker may have to experience ambiguity, and must be courageous: **In spiritual life it is not necessary to have a complete map of the Path in order to begin travelling. On the contrary, insistence upon having such complete knowledge may actually hinder rather than help the onward march. The deeper secrets of spiritual life are unravelled to those who take risks and who make bold experiments with it. They are not meant for the idler who seeks guarantees for every step. He who speculates from the shore about the ocean shall know only its surface, but he who would know the depths of the ocean must be willing to plunge into it.**[16]

If Meher Baba's description of existence is correct, every soul, in one lifetime or another, will reach a point where it can advance its spiritual development consciously. From Baba's perspective, that time cannot come too quickly.

Sooner or later, man must look within, ponder deeply and search within his own heart for those factors which hold him down in spiritual thraldom; and sooner or later, he must break asunder the gnawing chains of separative thinking which keeps him away from the immense and limitless life of the spirit to which he is the rightful heir.

Then why not sooner, rather than later? *Now* is the time to cast off the veil of imagined duality and unreservedly surrender to the life of open and undisguised love which is pure and selfless and which knows no fear and needs no apology.[17]

PART II

General Methods

Introduction

Dear Reader,

Part II launches into the pragmatics of the search, the general methods for attaining spiritual growth. I call the methods general because they form the core of all applied mysticism, Eastern and Western, historical and contemporary. Chapters 3, 4, and 5 describe three primary spiritual approaches—the paths of knowledge, love, and action. They form the background for the more specific method unique to Meher Baba, but are also relevant for any spiritual orientation. Although these general methods have distinct qualities, Baba reminds aspirants, **In the end, all walks of life and all paths ultimately lead to the one goal, which is God. All rivers enter into the ocean regardless of the diverse directions in which they flow, and in spite of the many meanderings they may take.**[1]

No great journey occurs without obstacles and directional confusion. The experiential terrain of inner space can be very baffling. Part II ends with Chapter 6, in which Baba examines counterproductive or limiting trails and some pitfalls on the path—tempting pursuits that turn into spiritual blind alleys. But whether negative or positive, Baba's evaluation of various methods is never arbitrary, so I have chosen to begin this section with some of his general guidelines for assessing any available technique.

The Technology of Realization

According to Meher Baba, any spiritual method may be evaluated on its ability to accomplish two interrelated objectives: (1) it must help the aspirant to free consciousness from the accumulated impressions of illusion, and (2) it must also help diminish the limited "ego"—the cause of experienced separation from one's real Self.

Sanskaras *and Their Elimination*

Sanskaras, or "impressions," are the contents of consciousness, one's accumulated thoughts, feelings, and sensations, like layers of dust on a perfect mirror: **Human beings do not have Self-illumination, because their consciousness is shrouded in *sanskaras* or the accumulated imprints of past experience. In them the will-to-be-conscious with which evolution started has succeeded in creating consciousness. But it does not arrive at the knowledge of the Oversoul, because the individual soul is impelled to use consciousness for experiencing *sanskaras* instead of utilising it for experiencing its own true nature as the Oversoul.[2]**

The power and effect of impressions can hardly be overestimated. An impression is solidified might, and its inertness makes it immobile and durable. . . . The mind contains many heterogeneous *sanskaras* and, while seeking expression in consciousness, they often clash with each other. The clash of *sanskaras* is experienced in consciousness as a mental conflict. . . . Experience can become truly harmonious and integral only when consciousness is emancipated from the impressions. . . . The problem of deconditioning the mind through the removal of *sanskaras* is therefore extremely important.[3]

This deconditioning process, the release from binding impressions, takes place in five ways:

(1) *The cessation of new sanskaras.* This consists in putting an end to the ever-renewing activity of creating fresh *sanskaras.* If the formation of *sanskaras* is compared to the winding of a string around a stick, this step amounts to the cessation of the further winding of the string.

(2) *The wearing out of old sanskaras.* If *sanskaras* are withheld from expressing themselves in action and experience, they are gradually worn out. In the analogy of the string, this process is comparable to the wearing out of the string. . . .

(3) *The unwinding of past sanskaras.* This process consists in annulling past *sanskaras* by mentally reversing the process which leads to their formation. Continuing our analogy, it is like unwinding the string.

(4) *The dispersion and exhaustion of some sanskaras.* If the psychic energy which is locked up in *sanskaras* is sublimated and

diverted into other channels, they are dispersed and heaved and tend to disappear.

(5) *The wiping out of sanskaras.* This consists in completely annihilating *sanskaras.* In the analogy of the string, this is comparable to cutting the string with a pair of scissors. The final wiping out of *sanskaras* can be effected only by the grace of a Perfect Master.[4]

The Ego and Its Termination

If impressions are the limiting *contents* of consciousness, the ego is the limiting *structure* of consciousness. This bunch of consolidated impressions, the ego, the false self, the focus of duality, is the ultimate obstacle for the mystic aspirant.

The formation of the ego serves the purpose of giving a certain amount of stability to conscious processes and also secures a working equilibrium which makes for a planned and organised life.[5] While provisionally serving a useful purpose as a centre of consciousness, the ego, as an affirmation of separateness, constitutes the chief hindrance to spiritual emancipation and enlightenment of consciousness.[6] The ego thus marks and fulfills a certain necessity in the further progress of consciousness. But since the ego takes shelter in the false idea of being the body, it is a source of much illusion. . . . It is of the essence of the ego that it should feel separate from the rest of life by contrasting itself with other forms of life. Thus, though inwardly trying to complete and integrate individual experience, the ego also creates an artificial division between external and internal life in the very attempt to feel and secure its own existence.[7]

In actuality, God is not far from the seeker, nor is it impossible to see Him. He is like the sun, which is ever shining right above you. It is you who have held over your head the umbrella of your variegated mental impressions which hide Him from your view. You have only to remove the umbrella and the Sun is there for you to see. It does not have to be brought there from anywhere. But such a tiny and trivial thing as an umbrella can deprive you of such a stupendous fact as the Sun.[8]

Thus, one criterion of effective spirituality is the slimming down of the ego, the disintegration of "selfishness." **The disintegration of the ego culminates in realising the Truth. The false nucleus of con-**

solidated *sanskaras* must disappear if there is to be a true integration and fulfillment of life.[9]

From this frame of reference, we are able to understand what the great mystics meant by such terms as "ego-death," "the death of the false self," and "rebirth."

Jesus, Buddha, Muhammad, Zoroaster, all meant what I mean by real birth and real death. I say you are born once and die once. All the so-called births and deaths are only sleeps and wakings. . . . You never die. Only the blessed ones die and become one with God.[10]

We must lose ourselves in order to
find ourselves.
Thus loss is gain.
We must die to self in order to
live in God.
Thus death is life.[11]

There is therefore a logic to the ineffable; progress toward conscious enjoyment of reality depends upon the gradual exhaustion of limiting impressions and the destruction of the separative ego. To the extent that the general methods of knowledge, love, and action accomplish this, they become **transmuted into a path of living discovery by having become the focal point of the aspirant's entire being.**[12]

CHAPTER 3

The Path of Knowledge

When mind soars in pursuit of the things conceived in space, it pursues emptiness; but when man dives deep within himself, he experiences the fullness of existence.

—MEHER BABA, *Universal Message*

The way of knowledge (dnyana-marga) is one of the principal routes by which the individual may start a spiritual journey. The object of this path is not knowledge derived merely by the intellect, but a kind of wisdom that utilizes the faculties of the higher mind. Starting perhaps with intellectual inquiry, it eventually moves to an understanding that goes beyond categories. In this method an aspirant tries to control, focus, and train his consciousness for the attainment of spiritual freedom. Describing the major facets of this *sadhana* (technique of attainment), Baba writes, **The *Sadhana* of knowledge finds its expression through (*a*) the exercise of detachment which is born of true understanding, (*b*) the different forms of meditation and (*c*) the constant use of discrimination and intuition.**[1]

Giving further explanation about detachment, Baba states, **The individual soul is entangled in the world of forms and does not know itself as part and parcel of the being of God. This ignorance constitutes the bondage of the soul, and spiritual *Sadhana* must aim at securing emancipation from this bondage. External renunciation of things of this world is therefore counted among the *Sadhanas* which lead to liberation. Though such external renunciation may have its own value, it is not absolutely necessary. What is**

needed is internal renunciation of craving for the things of this world. When craving is given up it matters little whether the soul has or has not externally renounced the things of this world, because the soul has internally disentangled itself from the illusory world of forms and has prepared itself for the state of *Mukti* [Liberation]. **Detachment is an important part of the *Sadhana* of Knowledge.**[2]

Baba also describes the key role of discrimination and intuition. **Infinite knowledge is latent in everyone but it has to be unveiled. The way to increase knowledge is to put into practice that bit of spiritual wisdom which a person may happen to have. The teachings which have come to humanity through the Masters of wisdom, and the inborn sense of values which the aspirant brings with himself, shed sufficient light upon the *next* step which the aspirant has to take. The difficult thing is to act upon the knowledge which he has. One of the best methods of adding to one's own spiritual wisdom is to make use of the knowledge which one already has. If *Sadhana* of knowledge is to be fruitful it must be implemented at every step by due emphasis on action. Everyday life must be guided by discrimination and inspired by the highest intuitions.**[3]

Before exploring Baba's explanation of meditation, let us examine the nature of traditional yoga, since yogic techniques usually require the control and discipline of the mind.

Discipline and Knowledge: Traditional Yoga

The common conception of yoga can evoke the image of bearded ascetics meditating pretzel-legged in mountain caves. But from Meher Baba's perspective, all yogas (bhakti, karma, etc.) are simply different ways of trying to see and become one with God. One traditional yogic approach (the way of mental and physical discipline) has three main systems:

(1) *Hatha Yoga*, which consists of self-mortifying ascetism and physical austerities; (2) *Raja Yoga*, which is the process of mental self-denial through resistance to all desires; and (3) the positive system of *Pranayama*, which consists in the awakening of the *Kundalini*, and meditation through an ascending order of exercises. It

is characteristic of all the different systems of yoga that they emphasize the purification and preparation of bodies or vehicles of consciousness, rather than concerning themselves directly with the onward movement of consciousness itself. The contribution of yoga is comparable to that of a physician who removes the ailments which have developed in the functioning of the internal organs of the body.

Of the different systems of yoga, *Hatha Yoga* is the most superficial. The self-imposed austerities represent in a sense a pressuring of God, or of a God-realized Master, for either power or realization. It is a kind of bargaining in which penance is undertaken with an ulterior motive. It can hardly be called self-sacrifice, for the things apparently denied oneself are denied in order that one might have something else. Ultimately it reduces to intelligent selfishness.

Spirituality, as love, can never be achieved through any type of coercion. If spiritual attainment should be sought in this manner, the person invites harm upon himself rather than spiritual benefit, and restriction of power rather than expansion. In brief, he gets exactly the opposite of what he sought.

The yoga of mental self-denial through resistance to all desires *(Raja Yoga)* is chiefly negative in its method. It consists in a concentrated attempt to be freed from all good and bad wants which plague the mind. In following this method the individual attempts to avoid all wants and desires. This in itself is a form of wanting, for it is wanting a state of wanting nothing. However, this form of yoga, when carried to its extreme limit, can result in the subjective annihilation of the ego-structure of desires.

The positive system of yoga consisting in the practice of *Pranayama* (breathing exercises) gives increased control over *prana* or the vital energy. It also includes the awakening of the *Kundalini* or the latent spiritual power in man, and is supplemented by an ascending order of meditation exercises. But in yoga there is the danger of the aspirant having a "fall" and retrogressing spiritually if he misuses his awakened occult powers.[4] Baba recommends that aspirants avoid this type of yoga unless under the direct supervision of a master who has transcended all the temptations of occult powers. Otherwise, a fall is very likely.

Meditation

Although frequently misinterpreted and misapplied, meditation is central to the path of knowledge. In Volume II of the *Discourses,* Meher Baba gives a comprehensive analysis of the nature, functions, types, and practice of meditation.

Baba sees meditation as a very general process, to be narrowed down for spiritual purposes: **Meditation is another means through which spiritual knowledge is sought. Meditation should not be regarded as some queer pursuit peculiar to dwellers in caves. Every person finds himself meditating on something or another. The difference between such natural meditation and the meditation of the aspirant is that the latter is systematic and organised thinking about things that have spiritual importance.**[5]

Such deep meditation on spiritual realities is aimed at assimilating their inner meaning, and results in lifting them out of the category of intellectual playthings into animating principles which invade and gradually transmute the innermost core of the aspirant.[6]

So, generally, meditation is an intense attempt at understanding experience by focusing on spiritual themes. Baba notes that **the object of meditation has always to be carefully selected and must be *spiritually important;* it has to be some divine person or object, or some spiritually significant theme or truth. In order to attain success in meditation the mind must not only get interested in the divine subjects or truths, but must also begin by trying to understand and appreciate them. . . .**

In concentration as well as in meditation, there is a peaceful intermingling of love and longing for the divine object or principle on which the mind dwells, and both these psychic activities are very different from the merely mechanical processes which have rigid regularity and unrelieved monotony. . . .

Meditation should not be resorted to with a heavy heart, as if one were taking castor oil. One has to be serious about meditation, but not grave or melancholy. Humour and cheerfulness not only do not interfere with the progress of meditation but actually contribute to it.[7]

In his analysis of formal meditation, Baba gives additional

technical hints. He suggests the value of relative silence and solitude, the desirability of darkness or closing one's eyes, the use of any comfortable and relaxed position that minimizes physical tension and pain without encouraging sleep, and the standardization of the position, spot, and hour of meditation.

A problem for most meditators is learning the correct technique for handling disturbing thoughts. **The first principle which aspirants have to remember is that the mind can be controlled and directed in meditation only according to laws inherent in the make-up of the mind itself, and not by means of the application of any mechanical or semi-mechanical force. . . . It is useless to waste psychic energy by trying *directly* to combat and repress disturbing thoughts. . . . It is best to ignore them and turn to the object of meditation as early as possible without attaching any undue importance to the disturbing factors . . . it becomes possible to let the disturbing thoughts die through sheer neglect, thus making the mind permanently steady in the object of meditation.**[8]

Chief Types of Meditation

As set forth in Volume II of the *Discourses* (pp. 111–175), the kinds of spiritually relevant meditation are various and complex. Broadly, Meher Baba includes *meditation of the heart* and *meditation of action* in his definition, but most of his discussion revolves around *discriminative* meditation, the type usually associated with the path of knowledge.

Baba describes at least eighteen categories of meditative practice, beginning with the varied forms of meditation before a person becomes an aspirant. An aspirant may embark upon general meditation (the assimilation of the Divine Truth) or specialized meditation (which selects some definite items of experience). General meditation can include philosophical thinking, hearing a discourse directly from a Master, or reading the written expositions of the Masters. Specialized meditation may be *personal* or *impersonal.* Personal meditation concerned with the *objects* of experience would include meditation on the divine qualities of the Master and concentration on the form of the Master.

Impersonal meditation concerned with the objects of experience includes meditation regarding the numerous forms of manifested life, meditation regarding one's own bodies, and meditation on the formless and infinite aspect of God. Baba mentions two forms of impersonal meditation concerned with the *subject* of experience—quest for the agent of action and considering oneself as the witness. Finally, he describes the technique and difficulty of meditation concerned with *mental operations*—writing down thoughts, watching mental operations, and making the mind blank.

Aside from the major typologies, Baba distinguishes between *associative* and *dissociative* meditations. Ultimately, he sees associative meditations (for example, "I *am* infinite") as more valuable than the dissociative varieties (for example, "I am not my body"): **If a person is surrounded by shadows, it does not help very much to be continuously upset about them. If he has no interest except that of being cross with the shadows, there will be no end to his worries. But if, instead of fretting and fuming about the engulfing shadows, he sets himself to the more important task of bringing himself under the full blaze of the sun, he will discover that all the shadows have disappeared.**[9]

The Limitations of Meditation

Although it is possible to make substantial spiritual progress through appropriate meditations done properly, Baba warns that **The type of meditation necessary in a particular situation often cannot be correctly ascertained by the aspirant for himself. The aspirant can get addicted to one type of meditation so exclusively that he finds it difficult to get out of the groove which has been cut into his mind by the type of meditation he has been practising. He fails to see the importance of any other type of meditation and is not drawn by it. . . . if the aspirant takes to any type of meditation on his own initiative and without having the benefit of the guidance and supervision of the Master, he may get into it so far that he loses his perspective and is unable to recover himself.**[10]

Meditation may be very helpful to aspirants on the path. However, formal meditation of the mind can be supplanted by a more powerful focus.

I attach more importance to *love* and *work* than to meditation. If you love a person, you naturally and spontaneously think about

him. There is no question of forcing the mind into such meditation.[11]

Love is meditation in its highest form, but only that love which does not forget the Beloved for a single moment. Then meditation is not necessary. It is superfluous.[12] Love without meditation is enough—meditation without love is not. That is why Sadgurus or Perfect Masters do not set meditation for their disciples as a necessary routine. Rather, they stress the aspect of love and selfless service. The masters of the Path [limited teachers], on the other hand, not having reached the Goal themselves, advocate meditation to the aspirants following them.[13]

CHAPTER 4

The Path of Love

The true lover is born only at that moment when he dies for God. . . .

—MEHER BABA, quoted in Irani, *Family Letters*

Being is dying by loving.

—MEHER BABA, *Discourses*

Love might be called the heart of the spiritual path, but many religions and philosophies have trapped the mystic concept of love in hollow cliché. Love is absolutely central to the way of Meher Baba—as a potent method, not as superficial sentimentality.

The Nature of Love

To Meher Baba, the real nature of love is intimately connected with the very deepest instincts of consciousness; in one sense, it *is* the will-to-be-conscious.

Life and love are inseparable from each other. Where there is life, there is love. Even the most rudimentary consciousness is always trying to burst out of its limitations and experience some kind of unity with other forms. Though each form is separate from other forms, in *reality* they are all forms of the same unity of life. The latent sense for this hidden inner reality indirectly makes itself felt . . . through the attraction which one form has for another form.

The law of *gravitation* . . . is in its own way a dim reflection of

the love which pervades every part of the universe. Even the forces of repulsion are in truth expressions of love, since things are repelled from each other because they are more powerfully attracted to some other things. . . . The forces of *cohesion* and *affinity* which prevail in the very constitution of matter are positive expressions of love. A striking example of love at this level is found in the attraction which the magnet exercises for iron. All these forms of love are of the lowest type, since they are necessarily conditioned by the rudimentary consciousness in which they appear.

In the animal world love becomes more explicit in the form of *conscious impulses* which are directed towards different objects in the surroundings. This love is *instinctive* and it takes the form of gratifying different desires through the appropriation of suitable objects. When the tiger seeks to devour the deer he is in a very real sense in love with the deer. Sex-attraction is another form of love at this level. All the expressions of love at this stage have one thing in common, viz., they all *seek to satisfy some bodily impulse or desire* through the object of love.[1]

As consciousness evolves through higher forms, so does the possibility of love: **Human love is much higher than all these lower forms of love because human beings have the fully developed form of consciousness. . . .** [But] **human love is encircled by a number of obstructive factors. . . . In one sense, even these obstructive factors are either *forms* of lower love or the inevitable *side-results* of these lower forms of love. Infatuation, lust and greed might be looked upon as perverted and lower forms of love. In infatuation a person is *enamoured* of a sensual object; in lust he develops a *craving* for sensations in relation to it; and in greed he desires to *possess* it. . . . greed has a tendency to extend from the original object to the *means* of obtaining it. . . . Infatuation, lust and greed constitute a spiritual malady which is often rendered more virulent by the aggravating symptoms of anger and jealousy. . . . Anger and jealousy come into existence when these lower forms of love are thwarted or threatened to be thwarted.**[2]

Baba explains that the lower forms obstruct the release of purer love, which is qualitatively different: **In infatuation, the person is a *passive victim* of the spell of conceived attraction for the object. In love there is an *active appreciation* of the intrinsic worth of the object of love. . . . in lust there is the *accentuation of separateness and suffering*, but in love there is the *feeling of unity and joy*.**

. . . Lust is a craving of the senses, love is the expression of the spirit. Lust *seeks* fulfillment but love *experiences* fulfillment. In lust there is *excitement*, but in love there is *tranquility*. . . . In greed the self tries to possess the object, but is itself possessed by the object. In love the self offers itself to the beloved without any reservations, but in that very act it finds that it has included the beloved in its own being. . . .

. . . in love there is an *expansion* in being. To have loved one soul is like adding its life to your own. Your life is, as it were, multiplied and you virtually live in two centres. If you love the whole world you vicariously live in the whole world. . . .[3]

The Problem of Sex

Meher Baba's analysis of physical sexuality goes beyond moralistic judgment. In his cosmology there is no personal "Satan," eternal hell, or absolute evil. Given the ultimate goal of God-realization, "good" is anything that frees consciousness to experience divine love; "evil" is anything which obstructs spiritual freedom. Baba views sexuality from this perspective, noting the spiritual limitations and possibilities in male-female relationships. To the extent that sexual contact reflects lust for sensation, it is a roadblock; to the extent that it is an expression of selfless love, it becomes more consistent with spiritual progress.

The craving for sexual sensation is a serious obstacle to spiritual development, but originates from understandable motives. Baba points out that identification with the male-female polarity is the most powerful experience of duality, that we reincarnate as both male and female, and that sexual attraction is **a result of the effort which the mind makes to unite with its own unconscious part.** But a purely physical solution to compensate for fragmentation is impossible because, **paradoxical though it may seem, the *form* of the opposite sex prevents the true understanding of *experience* associated with the opposite sex.[4]**

Baba thus states that relationships motivated primarily by physical desire tend to choke the development of real love. This spiritual roadblock is intensified by sexual promiscuity, in which **the temptation to explore the possibilities of mere sex contact is formidable.**

. . . In promiscuity the suggestions of lust are necessarily the first to present themselves to the mind, and the individual is doomed to react to people within the limitation of this initial perversion and thus close the door to deeper experiences.[5]

The problem of sensual desire can haunt the aspirant all along the spiritual path in both obvious and subtle forms. Baba advances two different kinds of solutions, the first occurring when a seeker gets fed up with both indulgence and repression and learns detachment. **When the aspirant becomes fully awake to the inevitable bondage and suffering entailed by craving, he begins voluntarily to disburden himself of craving through intelligent understanding.**[6]

Perhaps a more palatable solution is the sublimation of physical desire. **This lust must be converted into love. What is lust, but a craving to satisfy physical senses, and love is the craving of the soul.**[7] In all practicality, Baba advises a committed aspirant to follow either strict celibacy or marriage, whichever is more natural. He suggests lifetime celibacy only for those serious pilgrims to whom restraint comes easily, its value lying **in the habit of restraint and the sense of detachment and independence which it gives.**[8]

In parallel, Baba points out the immense possibilities for spiritual growth in a totally committed two-person relationship: **The value of marriage lies in lessons of mutual adjustment and the sense of unity with the other. . . . In one sense married life may be looked upon as the intensification of most human problems. As such it becomes the rallying ground for the forces of bondage as well as the forces of freedom, the factors of ignorance as well as the factors of light. . . . In married life two souls get linked in many ways, with the result that they are called upon to tackle the whole complex problem of personality rather than any simple problem created by some isolated desire.**[9]

In the beginning of married life the partners are drawn to each other by lust as well as love, but with conscious and deliberate cooperation they can gradually lessen the element of lust and increase the element of love. Through this process of sublimation lust ultimately gives place to deep love. By the mutual sharing of joys and sorrows the partners march on from one spiritual triumph to another, from deep love to ever deeper love, till the possessive and jealous love of the initial period is entirely replaced by a self-giving and expansive love. In fact, through the intelligent handling

of marriage a person may traverse so much of the spiritual path that it needs only a touch by the Master to raise him into the sanctuary of eternal life.[10]

Love as a Spiritual Method

Knowledge and love both have many forms. As a spiritual method, the way of knowledge requires the focus and control of the higher mind. The way of love demands refinement of higher emotions. In this perhaps highest of the general methods, **The sojourn of the soul is a thrilling divine romance in which the lover, who in the beginning is conscious of nothing but emptiness, frustration, superficiality and the gnawing chains of bondage, gradually attains an increasingly fuller and freer expression of love, and ultimately disappears and merges in the divine Beloved to realise the unity of the Lover and the Beloved in the supreme and eternal fact of God as Infinite Love.**[11]

The special potency of love in liberating consciousness comes from its ability to deal with the dual problems of limiting *sanskaras* and the separative ego: **In love the soul is completely absorbed in the Beloved and is therefore detached from the actions of the body or mind. This puts an end to the formation of new *sanskaras* and also results in the undoing of old *sanskaras* by giving to life an entirely new direction. Nowhere does self-forgetfulness come so naturally and completely as in the intensity of love. Hence it has been given the foremost place among the methods which secure release of consciousness from the bondage of *sanskaras*.**[12]

All experiences—small or great—and all aspirations—good or bad—create a load of impressions and nourish the sense of the "I." The only experience which makes for the slimming down of the ego is the experience of love, and the only aspiration which makes for the alleviation of separateness is the longing to become one with the Beloved. Craving, hatred, anger, fear and jealousy are all exclusive attitudes which create a gulf between oneself and the rest of life. . . . In seeking or experiencing union with the Beloved the sense of the "I" becomes feeble. In love the "I" does not think of self-preservation, just as the moth is not at all afraid of getting burnt in the fire. The *ego* is the affirmation of being *separate from*

***the other*, while *love* is the affirmation of being *one with the other*. Hence the ego can be dissolved only through real love.**[13]

When love is deep and intense it is called *Bhakti*, or devotion. In its initial stages devotion is expressed through symbol-worship, supplication before the deities and reverence and allegiance to the revealed scriptures, or the pursuit of the Highest through abstract thinking. In its more advanced stages devotion expresses itself as interest in human welfare and the service of humanity, love and reverence for saints and allegiance and obedience to the spiritual Master. These stages have their relative values and relative results.[14]

On Loving God

How can love be applied for the greatest spiritual benefit? Perhaps a hint can be taken from Baba's discourses on meditation: the *object* of meditation may be more important than the *process*. In the same way that the mind tends to become like its object of thought, consciousness tends even more to become what it loves. Thus, the spiritual aspirant can do no better than to love his highest goal—God. **Love God, and you will find that your own self is nothing but God.**[15] **The only answer is Love. If we love God, we become Him. There is no further question. But we must love with all our hearts, so that only God exists for us.**[16]

But even if the aspirant sees loving God as his highest priority, how does he do it? Baba suggests that it cannot be forced or derived from religious frenzies. Divine love is much more complex and deep than superficial emotion. **God does not listen to the language of the tongue and its *japs*, *mantras*, devotional songs and so on. He does not listen to the language of the mind and its routine meditations, concentrations and thoughts about God. He only listens to the language of the heart and its message of love, which needs no ceremony or show, only silent devotion for the Beloved.**

This love can be expressed in various ways, all of which ultimately result in union with God.[17]

In the later stages of the path, the aspirant-lover becomes more and more consumed by longing to unite with his beloved God. This bittersweet spiritual obsession is beautifully expressed in the mystic

Sufi poetry of Hafiz and others. But for the aspirant at earlier stages, **Beloved God is in all. What is then the duty of the lover? It is to make the Beloved happy without sparing himself. . . . The only thought a lover of God should have is to make the Beloved happy. Thus if you stop thinking of your own happiness and give happiness to others, you will then indeed play the part of the lover of God, because Beloved God is in all.**[18]

Real love can be expressed in various ways, Baba writes, and they all ultimately result in union with God; but **The practical way for the average man to express love is to speak lovingly, think lovingly and act lovingly towards all mankind, feeling God to be present in everyone.**[19]

This longing to love is eventually expressible in the ordinary world and becomes manifest in relation to others: **The more you remember others with kindliness and generosity, the more you forget yourself; and when you completely forget yourself, you find God.**[20]

How to love God? **If we understand and feel that the greatest act of devotion and worship to God is not to hurt or harm any of His beings, we are loving God.**

To love God in the most practical way is to love our fellow beings. If we feel for others in the same way as we feel for our own dear ones, we love God.

If, instead of seeing faults in others, we look within ourselves, we are loving God.

If, instead of robbing others to help ourselves, we rob ourselves to help others, we are loving God.

If we suffer in the sufferings of others and feel happy in the happiness of others, we are loving God.

If, instead of worrying over our own misfortunes, we think of ourselves [as] **more fortunate than many many others, we are loving God.**

If we endure our lot with patience and contentment, accepting it as His Will, we are loving God.[21]

To love God as He should be loved is no easy trick, but a gift that can be received only from an enlightened guru. However, once love is gained, it can be redistributed. **Love is essentially self-communicative; those who do not have it catch it from those who have it. . . . True love is unconquerable and irresistible. It goes**

on gathering power and spreading itself until eventually it transforms everyone it touches.[22]

Given the immense potency of love as a method, it is easier to understand why Baba might say, **Love is therefore rightly regarded as being the most important avenue leading to the realisation of the Highest.**[23] It is also easier to understand the mystic awe and wonder associated with the great saints and Masters who walked the way of love. In Part III, Baba takes the path of love one step further. As a prelude, he promises that:

> **LOVE CAN MAKE YOU**
>
> **1. Unlearn all that you have learned intellectually. Not remember the past, forget the present and not think of the future.**
>
> **2. Renounce everything and everyone including your own self.**
>
> **3. Escape from all that is illusory and take refuge in Reality.**
>
> **4. Burn all your desires and longings and kindle the one and only desire and longing—union with the Divine Beloved.**
>
> **5. Become God, live God's life and make others God unto yourself.**

To be worthy of the Divine gift of this love, let all your thoughts, words and deeds be controlled by the constant remembrance of God.[24]

CHAPTER 5

The Path of Action

God cannot be explained. . . . God can only be lived.

—MEHER BABA, *God Speaks*

Applied love *is* selfless action. Indeed, all the general paths are interrelated: spiritual wisdom leads to love for God; love inspires toward right action; enlightened action evokes increasing knowledge; and so forth. However, the aspirant treading the path of action places priority on *behavior* over *thought* or *feeling*. The way of action (karma-yoga, karma-marga) concentrates on the physical activities of the aspirant, his relationship to the world, and his mastery of the art of living.

Action is tangible; it goes beyond ideas, concepts, and superficial feelings. It is perhaps the truest measure of applied mysticism. Spirituality is not spirituality unless it is applied. ***Karma Yoga*, or the Path of Action, consists in acting up to the best intuitions of the heart without fear or hesitation. In *Sadhana* what counts is *practice* and not mere *theory*. . . . Thus a person who is not very learned but who sincerely takes the name of God and does his humble duties wholeheartedly, may actually be much nearer to God than one who knows all the metaphysics of the world but who does not allow any of his theories to modify his everyday life.[1] It is very simple. Let your head respond to the heart and then act accordingly.[2]**

Dealing with Impressions and Desires

The most solidified *sanskaras* are those produced by action in the physical body. The most pressing impressions are egoistic desires. Binding desires, composed of mental and emotional impressions, seek expression through action. Unfortunately, such action creates new impressions, which reinforce the desires, recharge the impulse to act, *ad infinitum*. Thus, the first phase in the path of action involves the aspirant's avoidance of behavior that binds him further.

Renunciation and Detachment

Ideally, one could shut off desires at their source, stopping the creation of new *sanskaras* by renunciation: **External renunciation means giving up completely all worldly delights and physical attachments to material things. . . . Internal renunciation means the control of desires at their very source so that the mind does not fall a prey to the demands of lust, greed and anger. . . . The fight is necessarily hard and long.**

For the West in particular, external renunciation is inadvisable and impracticable.[3] It is not the outward escape from the world that leads you to God. You have to live in the world, do all your duties, and yet feel as detached as if you were living in seclusion in the midst of intense activity. How can you renounce this body and mind by retiring into the jungles?[4]

Practically speaking, Baba says that internal renunciation is nearly impossible for the aspirant; lower desires will inevitably enter the mind. The next line of defense is to be relatively unaffected by these desires, to be detached. The pursuit of detachment occupies aspirants on both the path of knowledge and the path of action. The special goal of personal detachment is to neutralize impressions before they become overwhelming desires.

Baba often reminded disciples that detachment best occurs in ordinary life. **You may fast indefinitely, hang yourself upside down or knock out your brains on a slab or stone, and yet not free your mind of its impressions.**

Why then should you necessarily give up eating, drinking, doing your duty to your wife and children and looking after the welfare

of others? Such duties do not obstruct your way to the path at all. What *do* come in your way are the bindings which you create unnecessarily for yourself through attachment to the objects connected with those duties. You can own the world without being attached to it, so long as you do not allow yourself to be owned by any part of it.[5]

You only keep that which you let go. You have already lost a thing when you feel you have to hold it.[6] **He who does not want things, to him things come.**[7]

Sublimation and the Containment of Desires

Detachment is a fine goal but one that is difficult to attain. All but extraordinary seekers *are* powerfully affected by many desires. Understanding the difficulty fully, Baba offers another technique:

Even if a man has no control over the surging of desires, he can prevent them from being translated into action. . . . When desires arise and their release into action is barred, there is plenty of opportunity for spontaneous cogitation about these desires. This cogitation results in the wearing out of the corresponding *sanskaras*. . . . When desires are denied their expression and fulfillment in action and are allowed to pass through the intensity of the fire of a cogitative consciousness which does not sanction them, the seeds of these desires are consumed.[8]

Baba brings out the necessity of making conscious the undesirable contents of the unconscious, and he shows how they should be handled. **If no thoughts assail you, what is the difference between you and the stone that has no thoughts at all?**[9]

For the purification of your heart, leave your thoughts alone, but maintain a constant vigil over your actions. When you have thoughts of anger, lust or greed, do not worry about them and do not try to check them. Let all such thoughts come and go without putting them into action. Try to think counter-thoughts in order to discern, discriminate and learn. . . .[10]

This strategy might seem to run the risk of bottling up negative energy. However, **Control which has true spiritual value does not consist in the mechanical repression of thoughts and desires, but is the natural restraint exercised by perception of positive values discovered during the process of experience. . . . The process of replacing lower values by higher values is the process of sublima-**

tion which consists in diverting the psychic energy locked up in the old *sanskaras* towards creative and spiritual ends. When the psychic energy locked up in the *sanskaras* is thus diverted, they get dispersed and exhausted. The method of sublimation is the most natural and effective method of breaking through the grooves of old *sanskaras*. . . .[11] Baba specifically mentions meditation, selfless service of humanity, and devotion as possible channels for sublimation.

Whatever their lofty aspirations, most seekers treading the path of action find themselves doing things they should not. Along with possible lessons learned from mistakes, **The unwinding of many other *sanskaras* can be brought about through penance. This consists in augmenting and expressing the feeling of remorse which a man feels after realising that he has done some wrongful act. Repentance consists in mentally reviving the wrongs with severe self-condemnation. . . . Such penance unwinds the *sanskaras* which are responsible for the action. Self-condemnation accompanied by deep feeling can negate the *sanskaras* of anger, greed and lust. . . . It should, however, be carefully noted that there is always the danger in penance that the mind might dwell too long upon the wrongs done and thus develop the morbid habit of wailing and weeping over petty things. . . . Sincere penance does not consist in perpetuating grief for the wrongs, but in resolving to avoid in the future those deeds which call forth remorse.**[12]

Perfecting Action in the World

The control of desires and avoidance of selfish action is one phase of the path of action carried on within the aspirant himself. Another phase, the encouragement of positive action, usually has social components and renders the aspirant sensitive to ethics and service. Meher Baba sees morality as situational and dependent on motive, not as some intrinsic virtue or avoidance of sin. The value of positive acts resides both in the reduction of *sanskaras* and egoism and in the service to others.

Baba acknowledges that aspirants may well feel negative emotions toward others, but advises against acting on them. This helps to wear out undesirable impressions and avoids inviting the same in return. **If a person has done an evil turn to someone, he must**

receive the penalty for it and welcome the evil rebounding upon himself; and if he has done a good turn to someone, he must also receive the reward for it and enjoy the good rebounding upon himself. What he does for another, he has also done for himself, although it may take time for him to realize that this is exactly so.[13]

Tolerance and Honesty

One key ally on the journey of action is tolerance in its many forms—gentleness, fearlessness, and the acceptance of ignorance and hostility. **You can counteract a disease only by its antidote. Love is the antidote to hatred. When you feel like hating a man try to remind yourself that he is a form of your own Self.**[14]

Fear also is a subtle form of affirming separateness and . . . acts as a thick curtain between the "I" and the "you." . . . Therefore, not only other souls but God should be loved and not feared. To fear God or His manifestations is to strengthen duality; to love them is to weaken it.[15]

For real spiritual service the disciple has to be prepared for all eventualities. . . . When met with aggression he should be like the football that is kicked, for the very kicking raises it aloft and propels it onward till the goal is reached. . . . True humility is strength, not weakness. It disarms antagonism and ultimately conquers it.[16]

Related to tolerance is the ability to avoid unjust criticism of others. "Backbiting" is especially dangerous, **because this particular act or vice incurs the burden of sins, or what is technically termed as *sanskaras* of others, which is spiritually very derogatory and reactionary.**[17] **The habit of criticizing our fellow-beings is a bad one. At the back of it often lies self-righteousness, conceit, and a false sense of superiority. Sometimes it indicates envy, or a desire for retaliation.**[18] **Those who criticise should first look to themselves. They will find greater faults within themselves than in others.**[19]

Sincere self-examination is part of honesty, a quality much prized by Baba: **The truth of one's own perception and realization is the only road by which wholeness may be restored to the inner psychic being.**[20]

God is infinite honesty. To love God you must be honest.[21] **When**

hypocrisy comes into play it works much greater havoc within one's own psyche than in the outer sphere. The perceptible damage in the outer sphere is great, but the unperceived damage in the spiritual realm is stupendous.[22]

Selfless Service

Up to this point, it may seem to some readers that the path of action isn't much fun, that self-control may be virtuous but not especially fulfilling. However, a more rewarding aspect of the way of action is selfless service. The problems of control over desires diminish naturally as the ego is reduced by sincere concern for others.

As explained by Baba, an orientation toward selfless service should dominate the life of the aspirant on the way of action, which **may normally consist of a life of service to humanity, a life in which effort is expended to improve the well-being of people through social, political or physical projects. . . . Such service is not a mechanical response to a sense of duty, but a spontaneous expression of voluntary love. Through it man gradually becomes purer, is freed from many limitations, and finds peace of being as he becomes wholly detached from the results of his action.**[23]

Predictably, Baba shows how true selfless service dissipates *sanskaras* and weakens the false ego. **Since the soul is now centring its attention and interest not upon its own good, but upon the good of others, *the nucleus of the ego is deprived of its nourishing energy.* Selfless service is therefore one of the best methods of diverting and sublimating the energy locked up in the binding *sanskaras.*[24] Selfishness extended and expressed in the form of good deeds becomes the instrument of its own destruction. *The good is the main link between selfishness*[’s] *thriving and dying.*[25] When you are wholly occupied with the welfare of others you can hardly think of yourself.**[26]

The Practice of Selfless Service

Although there is great spiritual advantage in selfless service, Baba warns that good deeds should not be pursued blindly, especially when done unintelligently or for disguised ego enhancement.

Instead, service activities should be guided by spiritual understanding and should be an outcome of true love. True selfless servers are sensitive to the most subtle needs of humanity: ***They also serve who express their love in little things.*** **A word that gives courage to a drooping heart or a smile that brings hope and cheer in gloom, has as much claim to be regarded as service as onerous sacrifices and heroic self-denials. A glance which wipes out bitterness from the heart and sets it throbbing with a new love is also service, although there may be no thought of service in it.**[27]

Baba reminds the aspirant that selfless service may well result in benefit to others, but accrues a permanent advantage to oneself: **Never think you are obliging anybody by rendering any kind of help or giving anything in charity to him. On the contrary, believe that the recipient of your generosity gives you a chance to serve yourself.**[28]

Consistent with Meher Baba's priority on spiritual development, he sees one type of service as the highest: **Those who are inspired by the spirit of selfless service are quick to render unto humanity all possible help through the provision of the necessities of life like clothes and shelter, food and medicine, education and other amenities of civilization; and in pursuance of the Path of Duty, they are not only prepared to fight for defending the weak against cruel aggression and oppression, but also to lay down their very lives for the sake of others. All these types of service are great and good; but from the ultimate point of view, the help which secures Spiritual Freedom for humanity, surpasseth them all; and it is insuperable in importance.**[29] **The service which is concerned with spiritual understanding is the highest, because spiritual understanding includes the right perspective to all human problems and promotes their solution.**[30]

Regardless of whether a man is wealthy or poor, highly educated or illiterate, the only real help is to give him the perfect hope that everyone has a really equal opportunity to achieve everlasting freedom from all bindings.[31] **There is no gift greater than the gift of spiritual freedom and there is no task more important than that of helping others to attain it. . . .**[32]

The path of action has many facets—controlling lower desires from expression, developing spiritual traits, and directing energies toward selfless and intelligent service to others. In its highest expression it asks for both sacrifice and practicality. **Not by seeking** individual happiness or safety, but by again and again offering one's life in the service of others is it possible to rise to the unsurpassed completeness of realized truth. God is not to be sought by running away from life but by establishing unity with the one in the many.[33]

CHAPTER 6

Spiritual Sidetracks

Spiritual progress is like climbing through hills, dales, thorny woods, and along dangerous precipices to attain the mountain top. On this path there can be no halting or return. Everyone must get to the top, which is the direction of realization of the supreme Godhead. All hesitation, sidetracking or resting in halfway houses, or arguing about the best route, only postpones the day of final fulfillment.

—MEHER BABA, *Listen, Humanity*

Any of the general spiritual paths can take the aspirant to the very threshold of ultimate consciousness. Of course, each is subject to specific difficulties, including egoism, insincerity, and ignorance on the part of the seeker. Although Meher Baba stresses the positive when he discusses spiritual methods, he also lovingly warns new aspirants about techniques and experiences that are usually counterproductive. Seekers often pursue all sorts of psychic, occult, or esoteric practices hoping to enhance their life in some way. Some feel that these practices will aid their spiritual development; others use paranormal or mystical experiences as a measure of their progress.

Some inadequate approaches or phenomena are actually *harmful* (physically, mentally, or spiritually) to the aspirant's progress. Others might be relatively harmless but are *ineffective*, wasting the seeker's time and energy. Still other approaches or phenomena might be helpful and somewhat effective, but are inherently *limited* in progressing the aspirant beyond a certain point and may even confuse him about his spiritual status. Meher Baba has pointed out some of the most common spiritual sidetracks. In reviewing his advice, remember that Baba holds very high standards for spiritual methods, seeing complete fulfillment of the soul as the *only* true ultimate goal on the path.

Psychic and Occult Experience

Many persons have normally occurring "psychic experiences"—various forms of extrasensory perception, clairvoyance, precognition, and so forth. Meher Baba explains that these various psychic talents and senses are authentic, but that they have no inherent spiritual value.

Psychic or not, certain "occult" or "mystical" experiences may be expected to occur to most seekers at some point in their development. And since any new element may help or hinder the spiritual emancipation of consciousness, **the aspirant not only has to understand the value of such occult experiences as unusual and significant dreams, visions, glimpses of the subtle world and astral journeys, but also has to learn to distinguish such occult realities from hallucinations and delusions.**[1]

Baba advises a balanced attitude toward occult experiences. On the one hand, he asks aspirants not to dismiss them as mere mental illness; on the other, he cautions them against the far more common attitude of exaggerating their importance, **because the novelty and rarity of occult experiences are the factors which contribute to charging them with overwhelming importance. In fact, the ego of the aspirant tends to become attached to this new field revealed to him, and gives him the sense of being a rare person admitted to an exclusive privilege. The more experiences a person has the greater scope he desires. He also develops the habit of depending upon occult goading for each step on the Path, just as those who take drugs get addicted to them and require stimulation even for doing things which they could formerly do without such stimulation.**[2] **Getting enamored of such experiences is rawness** [immaturity] **on the Path.**[3]

Exalted experiences that result from intense spiritual practice can also be immensely overvalued. For example, hard work in yogic meditation may bring about a stilling of the mind and attendant peace called "samadhi," an experience held in awe by many spiritual teachers, but which Baba likens to intoxication followed by a headache. **If you have a brave heart and you patiently persist, then, in a few cases, the mind is temporarily stilled. Now this results in one of two things—one goes into a state of trance or one gets a sort of *samadhi*.[4] . . . one feels at peace with everything and everyone, and finally finds his mind still; but as soon as this *samadhi* is over, he is again his own ordinary self. Most yogis, after these *samadhi*, feel the strain of illusion even more.[5]**

The Case of Drugs

The attachment to illusory and limited experience has a contemporary symptom—the use of consciousness-altering chemical intoxicants. Needless to say, any psychoactive chemical that interferes with physical or mental functioning is no great boon to the spiritually inclined. Cultural experience has shown the inefficiency of using drugs to try to solve nonmedical problems. **Recourse to alcohol for drowning one's sorrows is the perverted form of solace. Solace afforded by things outside of you is synonymous with doping which gives a certain amount of relief or relaxation. Real and unalloyed solace is within you.[6] *Any* drug when used medically for diseases, under the direct supervision of a medical practitioner, is not impermissible and cannot be classed with individual usage of a drug for what one can get out of it—or hope to get out of it—whether thrills, forgetfulness, or a delusion of spiritual experience.[7]**

This latter delusion is especially interesting because of the explosion of drug use for spiritual purposes during the 1960s. Mind-changing, or "psychedelic," substances have been used in other cultures to stimulate religious experiences, and many Westerners, already preconditioned to the drug ethic, saw them as shortcuts to enlightenment. Meher Baba acknowledged that a few sincere seekers had aroused their spiritual longing while using consciousness-altering chemicals. However, he was explicit about the limits of drug-induced spirituality.

All so-called spiritual experiences generated by taking "mind-changing" drugs such as LSD, mescaline and psilocybin are superficial and add enormously to one's addiction to the deceptions of

illusion which is but the shadow of Reality. . . . The experience of a semblance of freedom that these drugs may temporarily give to one is in actuality a millstone round the aspirant's neck in his efforts towards emancipation from the rounds of birth and death.[8]

In personal conversation with a young American in 1967, Baba commented, **Many people in India smoke *ganja*** [marijuana] **and hashish—they see colors and forms and lights, and it makes them elated. But this elation is only temporary; it is a false experience. It gives only experiences of illusion and serves to take one farther away from reality. Indulgence in drugs is harmful physically, mentally and spiritually, and people should stop taking them. They bring more harm than good. Tell those ensnared in the drug-net of illusion to abstain.**[9]

Aside from the obvious physical, mental, and psychic risks, mind-altering chemicals have a profound ability to confuse the seeker.* It is somewhat like a dreaming man taking a dream capsule and experiencing that he is truly awake. In actuality, he is more deeply asleep than ever, although his illusory experience of wakefulness seems similar to the actual awake state. In other written communications, Baba indicated that the highest of all drug experiences reflect only the shadows of the next higher plane of consciousness. Thus, all considered, **It is absolutely essential for a spiritual aspirant who genuinely longs for union with God—the Reality—to shun experiments with the effects of certain drugs.**[10]

Occult Practices and Powers

Whereas some explorers seem most concerned with attaining experiences, others pursue practices for developing occult talents or powers. Often aspirants mistake these powers as signs of spiritual advancement, and too often they judge spiritual teachers by their

*Evidence grows about unusual psychic and "astral" symptoms from the use of mind-altering chemicals. Apparently, drugs can play havoc with the astral or semi-subtle body, prematurely opening up certain psychic centers and increasing vulnerability to "obsession" or "possession" by disembodied entities (commonly called spirits), some pretending to be spiritual guides. These side effects are parallel with the similar dangers of mediumism, the use of ouija boards, unsupervised practice of kundalini-yoga, and various forced techniques for psychic development. (A collection of such findings is being prepared for publication. Write to me care of Harper & Row for details.)

ability to perform physical and mental miracles. Baba confirms the existence of occult talents but insists that they have limited spiritual value.

Occult phenomena like stigmata, telekinesis (effecting the flight of objects . . . through the air), elongation, elevation, etc., may amuse, astound or overpower people. But they cannot bring about spiritual healing or uplift, which is the real thing that matters. They are just an illustration of the supersession of ordinary and known laws of nature by the supernatural and unknown laws of the inner spheres.[11] There are some [yogis] who can bodily walk on water or fly in the air without the aid of external means, and yet all this is no sign or proof of their having experienced divine love. Weighed on spiritual scales these miracles have no value whatsoever.[12] The curious might very well occupy their minds with these things, but they are best relegated to the background as insignificant. The real lover of Truth passes by these things without becoming entangled with any of them. He cannot afford to be distracted or diverted from his *real* objective, viz., attaining union with God and releasing the radiance of His purity and love.[13] From the spiritual point of view, an honest house-holder is a thousand and one times superior to the ascetic and mystic who works wonders by way of miracles without realising the Truth.[14]

When people desire occult powers for selfish motives, they risk personal and spiritual disaster. However, aspirants often gain powers naturally and legitimately in the course of gaining control over all the vehicles of consciousness. **Such control is made possible by the vivification and activation of unused *centres of control;* and the functioning of new centres brings in its train a number of occult powers. These new powers are commonly known as *siddhis,* and they can come before the aspirant has become spiritually perfect. In fact, egoism can flourish through the acquisition of such occult powers. The aspirant may not only take delight in possessing them, but might actually use them for mundane purposes from which he has not necessarily freed himself. *Siddhis* are therefore rightly regarded as obstacles to the attainment of realisation.[15]**

Obviously, occult powers in an egoless spiritual Master are used for the benefit of others. A sincere aspirant who gains powers in the course of spiritual development may progress if he uses them sparingly, compassionately, and wisely, without selfish motive.[16] But on the whole, occult powers are best avoided by the serious seeker.

False and Imperfect Teachers

Meher Baba puts considerable emphasis on the role of the teacher, the guide on the path. Yet he cautions that following a false or imperfect guru presents hazards all its own. In ordinary life, a poor guide is probably better than none at all. But in the jungle of spiritual ignorance, this is not necessarily so; indeed, a guide who himself is still lost can be worse than useless: **One's guru must be spiritually more advanced than oneself—better, if he is spiritually perfect. If you are in bonds and wish to be free, to whom should you go? Certainly to one who is quite free, and not to one whose hands are tied.**[17] **To entrust the development of your soul to the guidance of an imperfect teacher is like making a mad man sit on your chest with a sharp instrument in his hand.**[18]

Too often an aspirant judges a teacher by his possession of occult powers or by his ability to give the seeker "experiences." Serious seekers should ***Shun those masters who are like multi-colored electric signs that flash on and off, brightening the dark sky of your world for a moment and leaving you in darkness again.***[19] On visiting one Indian ashram, a young American saw a guru materialize a jeweled crucifix out of thin air before his very eyes. Asked about this fantastic and apparently authentic phenomenon, the wise student replied, "Well, I realized that if the guru was powerful enough to do *that,* he was certainly powerful enough to know that such a thing would impress us. And if he wanted to impress us in that way, I knew he couldn't be much of a guru."[20]

Perhaps the worst examples of imperfect masters are spiritual pretenders, those who pose as being spiritually advanced. **Even though I am the Ocean of compassion, I feel nauseated by the hypocritical saints and masters that now flourish everywhere like poisonous mushrooms.**[21] **One who indulges in happiness by allowing people to bow down to him without authority, feels the prick of conscience later on. And, with this feeling, he realizes that he has no authority, but has got so used to the habit of feeding his ego in this manner that he is unable to stop the practice. He continues indulging, and after a time does not pay heed to the pricks of conscience. He becomes numb to the voice within.**[22]

Less blatant is the teacher who is legitimately advanced but still has only imperfect knowledge. Here, karmic responsibility puts the guru in more spiritual danger than the credulous aspirant. Baba said that the motives of the seeker can rescue him: **A sincere belief, no matter how false, does not chain the seeker irredeemably because he is open to correction.**[23]

Although I cannot find confirming quotes in Baba's writings, let me suggest a distinction between an imperfect teacher's inspirational role and his responsibility for guidance. It may be that an imperfect teacher can help to the extent that he increases the seeker's motivation for the spiritual journey, inspiring him to further effort, alerting him to the possibility of something greater. In contrast, the taking of total responsibility for the disciple's life is appropriate only for Perfect Masters and the most advanced saints. Only a truly genuine teacher can reliably advise the aspirant on spiritual practices or deserve surrender, devotion, and commitment. Given these gifts by the well-meaning disciple, the imperfect teacher will most likely squander them because of limited vision. Perhaps that is why Baba "emphatically repeated that one must either follow one's creed or a Perfect Master, and what lies between is fraught with danger."[24]

PART III

Specific Techniques: The Way of Meher Baba

Introduction

Dear Reader,

The general paths to perfected consciousness are separate only in focus, not in principle. All aspirants can borrow from Meher Baba's lessons regarding knowledge, self-discipline, love, and action. Baba's insights in Part II can be adapted by almost anyone seeking enlightenment, no matter what technique is being used.

In their most exquisite execution, all the general paths lead one to the very brink of ultimate fulfillment. Needless to say, it is possible for an aspirant to exert all his energy on small facets of any one of them. Still, although laden with adventure and meaning, the spiritual journey is always difficult and occasionally treacherous.

Part III reviews a special aid that awaits a spiritual traveler. It describes the unique opportunities available through a Perfect Guide, one who knows all there is to know and who will assist an aspirant to proceed directly to his destination. The way of the Master is not inconsistent with the general methods; but, according to Meher Baba, it is a more efficient way to higher consciousness. In fact, very few are willing or ready to enter the "master game" described in Chapter 7. It calls for special commitments in a spiritual gamble for the highest stakes.

For those who follow a guide, relatively few are drawn to the inner path of the Avatar. Chapters 8 and 9 examine the Avataric technique as articulated by Meher Baba. In the pages that follow, I hope to illustrate what is involved in Meher Baba's path and how it can be carried forward by a willing aspirant.

The central theme is that a Master-disciple (teacher-student, lover-beloved) relationship with the Avatar offers a vehicle for profound spiritual progress. Chapter 10 stresses the qualities to be cultivated for perfecting such an internal relationship. Chapter 11 examines a special tool for cementing the relationship, the practice of remembrance. Finally, Chapter 12 summarizes Meher Baba's methods, expressed concretely by those who lived with him.

CHAPTER 7

The Way of the Master

> ***All talk about the path and the Goal is as a lantern carried by a blind man! A blind man needs a staff in his hand; the seeker needs his hand in God-Man's.***
>
> —MEHER BABA, quoted in Irani, *Family Letters*

The notion of a spiritual guide, teacher, guru, is foreign neither to Eastern nor Western mysticism. Spiritual aspirants have always looked for wise guides, whether the wiser teacher is called rishi or priest. The higher the teacher, the more useful is the guidance. However, an entire spiritual method is focused on a certain type of teacher, a perfect instructor, a true Master.

In *God Speaks*, Meher Baba explains that there are seven major planes or states of advanced consciousness beyond our ordinary awareness. They represent the "involution" of consciousness, the soul's increasing perception of Reality. As described by Baba, even the soul's experiences on the lower planes are ineffable to us. However, it takes a true saint, a teacher on the sixth plane of consciousness, seeing only God everywhere and in everything, to lead an aspirant reliably to God. Even such a great soul can raise only a few disciples to his own level; he cannot give God-realization. Only the seventh-plane Master (in the state of God-realization) is unlimited and takes the seeker from the very beginning to the very end of his spiritual trip.

The Perfect Guide

As Baba explains, a Perfect Guide is a soul who enjoys the ultimate state of consciousness—infinite wisdom, infinite power, and infinite bliss—and uses this state to help others advance spiritually. The most common appearance of a Perfect Guide is the Perfect Master.

After God-realization, some souls again descend or come down and become conscious of the whole creation as well as their gross, subtle and mental bodies, without in any way jeopardizing their God-consciousness. They are known as Perfect Masters. God as God alone is not consciously man, and man as man alone is not consciously God; the Man-God is consciously God as well as man.

By again becoming conscious of creation, the Man-God does not suffer the slightest deterioration of his spiritual status. What is spiritually disastrous is not *mere consciousness of creation,* but the fact that consciousness is *caught up* in creation because of the *sanskaras.* . . . Since the Man-God is free from all *sanskaras,* he is constantly conscious of being different from the bodies and uses them harmoniously as mere *instruments* for the expression of the Divine Will in all its purity.[1]

In the Man-God, the purpose of creation has been completely realised. He has nothing to obtain for himself by remaining in the world, yet he retains his bodies and continues to use them for emancipating other souls from bondage and helping them to attain God-consciousness.[2]

Baba explained that there are actually two types of Perfect Guides, the Perfect Master (Sadguru, Man-God, *Qutub*) and the reappearing Avatar (Christ, Messiah, God-Man). A Perfect Master is a soul who finishes evolution and then remains in the physical body; while **The foremost Sadguru who first emerged through evolution, and helped and helps other souls in bondage, is known as the Avatar. There is another difference between the Sadguru and the Avatar. When man becomes God and has creation-consciousness, he is called Sadguru (Man-God or Perfect Master). When God becomes man, he is called Avatar (God-Man or Messiah).[3]**

Metaphysically, such an idea may seem incredible; so we return to the analogy of the dream (limited consciousness) and the dreamer

(God). Most times, people are so identified with the characters in their dreams that they forget they are really one with the dreamer. Yet many have had an occasional experience of dreaming while being aware that they were dreaming. A Perfect Master is like a character in a dream who fully realizes he is also the dreamer. But he stays in the dream to help other characters wake up to their true identity.

The Role of a Master

Meher Baba's high estimation of the value of a Perfect Master has its roots in the criteria discussed previously. (Hereafter, I shall use the word "Master" to represent both a Perfect Master and the Avatar.)

Sanskaras *and the Ego*

The evolving soul is caught by its own limitations; the limited self can never destroy itself or its binding impressions. All actions of the ego, no matter how spiritual, create more impressions. Thus, the final removal of *sanskaras* must come from a source free from impressions.

The *Sadguru* can raise the aspirant from the ordinary intellectual level of consciousness to the level of consciousness where there is inspiration and intuition, and then onwards to the level of insight and illumination which culminates in his merging into the Infinite.[4] Because of his union with the Infinite, he is endowed with unlimited power and in the twinkling of an eye can annihilate all the *sanskaras* of the soul and liberate it from all entanglements and bondage.[5]

The principle is the same with the ego, which engages in a futile effort to annihilate itself through meditation, love, service, or whatever else. Baba has compared it with a man trying to stand on his own shoulders. Even when the aspirant makes considerable progress through independent effort, the "hydra-headed" ego stays alive. **In fact, in the more advanced stages of the Path, the ego does not seek to maintain itself through *open* methods but takes shelter in those very things which are pursued for the slimming down of the ego. These tactics of the ego are very much like guerilla warfare and are the most difficult to counteract. . . . Since the ego**

has almost infinite possibilities for making its existence secure and creating self-delusion, the aspirant finds it impossible to cope with the endless upcropping of fresh forms of the ego. He can hope to deal successfully with the deceptive tricks of the ego only through the help and grace of a Perfect Master.[6]

The Guidance of the Master

Although Baba says that total realization is impossible without the touch of a Perfect Master, the average reader is probably not a sixth-plane saint merely waiting for a Master to push him over the last gulf of illusion. For less advanced aspirants, although not necessary, a Master is extremely desirable.

The masses who try to attain the Truth by following rites and rituals are, as it were, in the goods [freight] **train which is detained indefinitely at various stations. Those who sincerely and devotedly meditate on God or dedicate their lives to the service of humanity are, as it were, in the ordinary train which stops at every station according to the time-table. But those who seek the company of the Truth-realized Master and carry out his orders in full surrenderance and faith are, as it were, in a special train which will take them to the goal in the shortest possible time, without halts at intermediate stations.**[7] **Since the Path lies through illusions of many kinds, the aspirant is never safe without the guidance of the Master who knows all the stages of the Path and can take him through them.**[8]

A Master works with his disciples in different ways at different times, but his methods are always effective. **Occasionally he may even do something which shocks others because it runs counter to their usual expectations. However, this is always intended to serve some spiritual purpose. The intervention of a short shocking dream is often useful in awakening a person from a long beautiful dream. Like the shocking dream, the shocks which the Man-God in his discretion deliberately administers, are eventually wholesome, although they may be unpleasant at the time.**[9]

Thus, a Master will produce varying feelings of inferiority and confidence in disciples, whichever might be required at a given time. Baba mentions also that a true Master grants occult experience to disciples only when necessary. Commonly, disciples spend some time in the physical presence of the Master. However, a Master's work is actually internal and is unaffected by physical distance or time.

The Role of the Aspirant

A Master's help may be constantly available, but it must also be received. Usually the aspirant, perceiving his helplessness, surrenders to the Master as his last and only resort. **This step, however, turns out to be more fruitful than all other measures which might have been tried for the slimming down and subsequent annihilation of the ego.**[10]

Once an aspirant has taken this step and is treading the path of the Master, his most fruitful attitude is one of attention and continuing surrender. **Complete surrender to the Divine Will of the Perfect One, and an unflinching readiness to carry out his orders rapidly, achieve a result not possible even by rigidly practising all the ethics of the world for a thousand years. The extraordinary results achieved by a Perfect Master are due to the fact that, being one with the Universal Mind, he is present in the mind of every human being and can therefore give just the particular help needed to awaken the highest consciousness latent in every individual.**[11]

In order to assist this process of surrender, Baba suggests that the aspirant concentrate his energy on the Master and try to replace the ego with the Master as the nucleus of his life. **The Master, when truly understood, is a standing affirmation of the unity of all life. Allegiance to the Master, therefore, brings about a gradual dissociation from the ego-nucleus which affirms separateness.**[12]

In practice Baba shows the aspirant how to avoid both inaction and pride of action by adopting **a provisional and working ego which will be entirely subservient to the Master. Before beginning anything, the aspirant thinks that it is not *he* who is doing it, but the Master who is getting it done through him. After doing it he does not tarry to claim the results of action or enjoy them, but becomes free of them by offering them to the Master. By training his mind in this spirit he succeeds in creating a new ego which, though pro-**

visional and working, is amply able to become a source of that confidence, feeling, enthusiasm and "go" which true action must express. This new ego is spiritually harmless, since it derives its life and being from the Master who represents Infinity. . . . The construction of a new ego which is entirely subservient to the Master is indispensable to the dynamics of spiritual advancement.[13]

Some people feel uncomfortable with the concept of dependence on a guru, but the existence of God-consciousness in human form is remarkably convenient for the aspirant. To love and relate to the impersonal aspect of God—God the infinite, beyond time and space, without form and attributes—is very difficult. Meditating on infinity might bend the aspirant's mind and little else. But when the infinite aspects of God are personalized in the Perfect Master or Avatar, then the mind and heart has a focus, a symbol that contains the whole.

Relevant here is the intricate question of Masters who have "died," sometimes called "dropping their bodies." Many seekers try to follow deceased guides and expect to be helped. In Baba's explanation of the working of the spiritual hierarchy, all saints and Masters, with the exception of the Avatar, give up their spiritual authority as soon as they leave their body. Their authority is usually transferred to another saint or Master in a physical body.

For example, a well-known and beloved spiritual figure is Sri Ramakrishna Paramahansa, who lived in India during the late 1800s. Meher Baba confirmed Ramakrishna's status as a Perfect Master but explained that such a Master no longer functions as a personal guide after his physical death.

Realization is the same for all. The differences among Prophets [Avatars] **and Perfect Masters lie not in the power, but in the authority to use it. That which is given by a Perfect Master to his chargeman is not power, but the authority to use it. A Perfect Master, strictly speaking, gives nothing to anybody. He merely shows the treasure that is within him. . . .**

No Perfect Master has authority to use his power after dropping his corporeal frame. Mind you! he has the power, but not the authority to use it. Wherever you see the tomb of a *Sadguru*, rest assured that there his power is. But if a devotee is benefited by worshipping there, never for a moment believe that the *Sadguru*

was the cause of his benefit. The devotee may merely be said to have utilized the power and thereby brought a blessing upon himself. A *Sadguru* can do good to others only so long as he lives in this gross world; after leaving his body he cannot make anybody cross a single plane [of consciousness], **and cannot wipe out anybody's *sanskaras;* though to those of his followers who call upon his infinite existence, his infinite state renders help according to the devotion behind the call.**[14]

For the aspirant seeking the incomparable guidance of a living Perfect Master, there is both good and bad news. First, the bad news: to come into physical contact with a living Master is nearly impossible because they are so few and so difficult to find. In *God Speaks,* Baba points out that there are only five Perfect Beings who function as Sadgurus at any one time on earth. Further, during Avataric periods (for example, much of the twentieth century), they tend to work behind the scenes and receive very little public attention. Indeed, as implied in Chapter 6, even finding an authentic saint is rare. Baba's sister and disciple, Manija S. Irani, once recalled, "Throughout the vast background of India's spiritual history there have been *rishis, maharishis,* yogis, *mahayogis, mahatmas,* gurus, . . . *sadhus* and the like. India still abounds with them. Like the shells swept ashore when the Tide comes in, at Avataric times they appear in profusion. A few among them are genuine. I recall how, when we were watching a conglomeration of 8,000 of them at Benares in 1939, Baba turned to us and gestured, **'Of these 8,000, only 8 are real.'**"[15]

Now for the good news: It is actually the Master's finding the disciple that counts. By means of their omniscience and spiritual agents, Perfect Masters are quite aware of advanced souls and draw such aspirants to them when the time is right.

No matter how unlikely such a meeting, seekers naturally might wonder what a Perfect Master would be like in the flesh. Meher Baba suggests that an open aspirant could notice three outstanding characteristics: a spontaneous love for all of creation without distinction; an undeniable atmosphere of bliss that radiates in his close vicinity; and a total adaptability and appeal to every level of humanity, learned or illiterate, rich or poor.

Of course, there are other tests for the possible quality of any spiritual teacher. When a pupil of a man who proclaimed himself to be a leading Master asked Baba, "Is he right to call himself such?" Baba replied: **Everyone has a right to call himself what he likes. It is for others to accept it or challenge it. It depends on his living, rather than his teachings.**[16] A seeker "shopping" for a highly developed spiritual teacher should be skeptical if the guru charges money for spiritual lessons, if his old and close disciples seem not to have made much progress, if his teachings are not internally consistent, if he asks for blind faith at the very beginning, if he allows an uncontrolled organization to be built around him, or if his methods cannot be applied to ordinary life.[17] Beyond such rational judgments the aspirant must use his intuition. Ultimately, if he decides to pursue some guru's path, he can still judge the method by its results for him.

In all probability the seeker on the way of the Master will not meet and follow a living Perfect Guide unless he is a very advanced soul. Usually, limited teachings and limited teachers must suffice. However, Meher Baba insists that there is always one access to an unlimited Master for the determined aspirant, no matter what his development. While Perfect Masters are mostly hidden by time and space, *the Avatar or God-Man is always accessible to everyone at any time in any place.* Baba describes the Avatar as that aspect of infinite God which relates directly to the universe and its developing souls and which occasionally incarnates in physical form to give lagging spirituality a push, simultaneously offering a unique path for personal development.

The easiest and safest way to lose one's finite ego is by surrendering completely to the Perfect Master or to the God-man (Avatar), who is consciously one with truth. . . . Of all the high roads which take the pilgrim directly to his divine destination, the quickest lies through the God-man (Christ, Messiah, Avatar). In the God-man, God reveals Himself in all His glory, with His infinite power, unfathomable knowledge, inexpressible bliss and eternal existence. The path through the God-man is available to all those who approach Him in complete surrenderance and unwavering faith. To the one who has unfaltering love for the God-man, the way to abiding truth is clear and safe. Such a one must waste no time playing with things that do not matter.[18]

The way of Meher Baba *is* the road of the Avatar.

CHAPTER 8

Meher Baba: Avatar and Guide

All religions of the world proclaim that there is but one God, the Father of all in creation. I am that Father.

—MEHER BABA, quoted in
Purdom, *The God-Man*

The way of Meher Baba is based on the possibility that the Avatar can function as a Perfect Guide for any willing aspirant.

According to Meher Baba, if he were merely an advanced soul or a great saint, that would mean he was not a Perfect Master. But even if he were a Perfect Master, he would no longer have the spiritual authority to help seekers because he has left his physical body. So the path of Meher Baba as personal spiritual Master is possible only if he is the Avatar, that Christ or God-Man who is the physical manifestation of God on earth. Meher Baba's method—the path of the God-Man—is absolutely dependent on his *being* the God-Man.

Meher Baba—God in human form? From a mystic point of view, we are all God. But Baba makes an extraordinary claim: that he is fully conscious of being God, has infinite power, wisdom, and bliss at his command, and is the reappearing Christ, the Prophet, Buddha, or Messiah.

The Appearance of the Avatar

According to Baba, the Avatar reappears on earth again and again, but he **is always one and the same because God is always one and the same.**[1]

The *Avatar* appears in different forms, under different names, at different times, in different parts of the world. As his appearance always coincides with the spiritual birth of man, so the period immediately preceding his manifestation is always one in which humanity suffers from the pangs of the approaching birth. Man seems more than ever enslaved by desire, more than ever driven by greed, held by fear, swept by anger. The strong dominate the weak; the rich oppress the poor; large masses of people are exploited for the benefit of the few who are in power. The individual, who finds no peace or rest, seeks to forget himself in excitement. Immorality increases, crime flourishes, religion is ridiculed. Corruption spreads throughout the social order. Class and national hatreds are aroused and fostered. Wars break out. Humanity grows desperate. There seems to be no possibility of stemming the tide of destruction.

At this moment the *Avatar* appears. Being the total manifestation of God in human form, he is like a gauge against which man can measure what he is and what he may become. He trues the standard of human values by interpreting them in terms of divinely human life.[2]

This *Avatar* was the first individual soul to emerge from the evolutionary process as a *Sadguru*, and he is the only *Avatar* who has ever manifested or will ever manifest. . . . Through him, periodically, God consciously becomes man for the liberation of mankind.[3]

Among the best known and honored manifestations of God as the Avatar, the earliest is Zoroaster. He came before Ram, Krishna, Buddha, Jesus and Mohammed.[4] . . . His [the Avatar's] physical presence among mankind is not understood and He is looked upon as an ordinary man of the world. When He asserts His divinity by proclaiming Himself the Avatar of the age, He is worshiped by some who accept Him as God, and glorified by a few who know Him as God on earth. It happens invariably though that the rest of humanity condemns Him while He is physically among them.[5]

In those that contact him he awakens a love that consumes all selfish desires in the flame of the one desire to serve him. Those who consecrate their lives to him gradually become identified with him in consciousness. Little by little, their humanity is absorbed into his divinity and they become free.[6]

Merwan Irani Revisited

Baba explained that God deliberately veils Himself in the physical body that contains the Christ until the appropriate time. Then, the five reigning Perfect Masters (who share infinite consciousness) prepare the world for the Avatar and assist in the unveiling process.

Before the Perfect Master Hazrat Babajan intervened,[7] Merwan Irani had very few hints about his destiny. Baba told of one such clue when Merwan was young: **One day, when a friend gave me a small booklet on the Buddha, I opened the book to the place that told about the second coming of the Buddha as Maitreya, the Lord of Mercy, and I realized all of a sudden, "I am that, actually," and I felt it deep within me. Then I forgot about it, and years passed by.**[8]

Recalling the sequence of events described in Chapter 1, the first phase of Merwan's unveiling gave him infinite consciousness of God but almost no consciousness of illusion. Since the Avatar must simultaneously experience the infinite consciousness of finiteness, Merwan's initial automaton-like bliss was soon replaced by intense agony as he was gradually pulled down to consciousness of illusion: **I did not want to come back to the ordinary . . . consciousness from that Blissful State where I alone was. But despite my resistance the five Perfect Masters kept "pulling me down" to ordinary consciousness for My destined Manifestation as Avatar. . . .**[9]

After becoming fully established as the Avatar in 1921, Meher Baba took direct command of the operation of the universe from the Perfect Masters,* as does every Avataric incarnation. As indicated in Chapter 1, three Perfect Masters publicly acknowledged this transition and Baba's authority.

* Hazrat Babajan of Poona, Sai Baba of Shirdi, and Upasni Maharaj of Sakori were mentioned previously. The two other Perfect Masters of the time were Tajuddin Baba of Nagpur and Narayan Maharaj of Kedgaon. There are eleven ages of varying lengths in an Avataric cycle. Every age has five Perfect Masters, but only the eleventh has an Avataric incarnation. The five Perfect Masters functioning today are not known by the editor; Baba said that they are rarely known to the public during an Avataric age.

Meher Baba on His Identity

In the early days Baba was regarded as "merely" a Perfect Master, but later he became explicit about his identity:

I am that Ancient One whose past is worshipped and remembered, whose present is ignored and forgotten and whose future (Advent) is anticipated with great fervour and longing.[10] I am God in human form.[11] I am the Ancient One, the Lord of the Universe.[12] There is no time and space for me, it is I who give them their relative existence. I see the past and the future as clearly and vividly as you see material things round about you.[13]

I assert unequivocally that I am infinite consciousness; and I can make this assertion because I *am* infinite consciousness. I am everything and I am beyond everything. I am ever conscious that I am in you, while you are never conscious that I am in you.[14] Believe that I am the Ancient One. Do not doubt that for a moment. There is no possibility of my being anyone else. I am not this body that you see. It is only a coat that I put on when I visit you. I am Infinite Consciousness. . . . Before me are saints and perfect saints and masters of the earlier stages of the spiritual path. They are all different forms of me. I am the Root of every one and every thing.[15]

In addition, Baba clearly identified himself as that same Avatar who manifested as previous incarnations of God: **I was Rama, I was Krishna, I was this One, I was that One, and now I am Meher Baba. In this form of flesh and blood I am that same Ancient One who alone is eternally worshipped and ignored, ever remembered and forgotten.[16]**

Krishna said that from time to time he came to protect his lovers. I am the Lord Krishna. I am the Christ, the personification of love.[17] I am the Christ. I know everything.[18]

When talking personally with his lovers, Baba reminded them that the Avatar is an integration of divinity and humanity, able to relate to every aspect of consciousness. **I am One with all on every level.[19] With a child I am a child; with the highest saints I am one with them. It is my nature to be absolutely natural, even with the beloved God, who is one with me, and I with him.[20]**

To some readers, such statements will appear at least immodest, if not downright arrogant. However, Baba emphasized that everyone is potentially God-conscious and that the real Meher Baba is no different from everyone's real Self:

Why is it that I am God and you are not God? It is because I am *conscious* that I am God, and you are not.[21] I tell you all with my divine authority that you and I are not "we," but "One." You unconsciously feel my Avatarhood within you. I consciously feel in you what each of you feels.[22] Be brave, be happy. I and you are one. And the Infinite that eternally belongs to me will one day belong to every individual.[23]

The Working of the Avatar

Because Meher Baba was explicit about his identity, he was asked countless questions about his previous Avataric incarnations. For instance, he was asked why different Avataric incarnations lived in different ways (for example, some married, some did not) or displayed varying emphases in their teachings.

Every Avatar adopts a particular aspect of his time. He adapts and embodies his mode of working according to the attitudes of the people.

The outstanding weakness that marked the attitude of the people in the time of Jesus was pomp, cruelty and pride; and to do away with that and set an example, he based his working or mode of life on simplicity, humility and suffering. And so there was no necessity for him to marry.

In the time of Mohammed, lust dominated in the minds of men, so much so that nearly every man used to have sex with several women. Mohammed, marking this point, made it lawful for every follower of his to have only a certain number of wives, and himself married seven . . . and so he fixed the number to seven from scores.

The people were too much steeped in materialism in the age of Buddha; therefore, stressing the nothingness of Maya, he set an example of true renunciation, and left his wife and children. He founded his system on renunciation. . . .

Dry atmosphere marked the age of Krishna. The predominating elements then were internal strife, jealousy, greed. So he

preached and founded his teachings on the gospel of love and gaiety, so that people began learning lessons in, and developing, love and merriment.

The hopelessness of the situation in Zoroaster's time, when people progressed neither materially nor spiritually, made him base his system . . . to make them live the life of the world, yet be spiritually inclined in search of God and Truth. . . . He founded his religion on the tenets of good thoughts, good words, good deeds.

The same, One Divine Element, had to give different teachings according to the different attitudes of the people in different times and in different circumstances. . . . God is One; but his manifestations at different times to satisfy the thirst (for Truth) ordains different ways and remedies.[24]

Meher Baba's Mission

What then is his Avataric task in *this* age?

Unity in the midst of diversity can be made to be felt only by touching the very core of the heart. That is the work for which I have come. . . . I have come to sow the seed of love in your hearts, so that, in spite of all superficial diversity which your life in illusion must experience and endure, the feeling of oneness, through love, is brought about amongst all the nations, creeds, sects and castes of the world.[25]

I have come to destroy in the world all rites and ceremonies that are superficial.[26] I am not come to establish any cult, society or organization; nor even to establish a new religion. The religion that I shall give teaches the Knowledge of the One behind the many. The book that I shall make people read is the book of the heart that holds the key to the mystery of life. I shall bring about a happy blending of the head and the heart. I shall revitalize all religions and cults, and bring them together like beads on one string.[27]

Baba gave one of his most powerful statements on his task for all humanity in 1958 as his "Universal Message":

I have come not to teach but to awaken. Understand therefore that I lay down no precepts. Throughout eternity I have laid down principles and precepts, but mankind has ignored them. Man's inability to live God's words makes the *Avatar's* teaching a

mockery. Instead of practising the compassion he taught, man has waged crusades in his name. Instead of living the humility, purity and truth of his words, man has given way to hatred, greed and violence. . . .

To get nearer and nearer to God you have to get further and further away from "I," "My," and "Mine." You have not to renounce anything but your own self. It is as simple as that, though found to be almost impossible. It is possible for you to renounce your limited self by my Grace. I have come to release that Grace.

I repeat, I lay down no precepts. When I release the tide of Truth which I have come to give, men's daily lives will be the living precept. The words I have not spoken will come to life in them. . . .

I am the Divine Beloved who loves you more than you can ever love yourself. . . .

All this world confusion and chaos was inevitable and no one is to blame. What had to happen has happened; and what has to happen will happen. There was and is no way out except through my coming in your midst. I had to come, and I have come. I am the Ancient One.[28]

Meher Baba's most important work was universal. By immersing himself in every bit of consciousness experienced in the world, the Avatar works to advance the spiritual status of all life. Baba's universal work, marked especially in his times of seclusion or fasting, took place on inner planes of consciousness, occasionally symbolized by his outer activities. Even though the Avatar is most concerned with humanity as a whole, he will work directly with individuals:

Besides giving a general push to the whole world, I shall lead all those who come to Me toward Light and Truth.[29] **The life in eternity knows no bondage, decay or sorrow. It is the everlasting and ever renewing self-affirmation of conscious, illimitable divinity. My mission is to help you inherit this hidden treasure of the Self.**[30]

Meher Baba's Silence

Meher Baba's mission of universal work was not limited by his silence. When Baba first began verbal silence in 1925, he told his disciples, **Hear well my voice; you will not hear it for a long time.**[31] Baba did not utter another physical word for the next forty-four years. When he was asked later why he kept silence, Baba explained that it was for several reasons: **Firstly, I feel that through you all, I am talking eternally. Secondly, to relieve the boredom of talking incessantly through your forms, I keep silence in my personal physical form. And thirdly, because all talk in itself is idle talk. Lectures, messages, statements, discourses of any kind, spiritual or otherwise, imparted through utterances or writings are just idle talk when not acted upon or lived up to.**[32]

But one reason for his silence seems to dominate all others in significance: **When I first began Silence, I knew that when I broke Silence, the world would know Me, and so I began.**[33] Meher Baba's comments on the breaking of his silence are among the most mysterious of his present advent. He alluded to a tremendous release of spiritual energy that would occur when he broke his silence and spoke a divine sound or "Word":

My present *avataric* Form is the last Incarnation of this cycle of time, hence my Manifestation will be the greatest. When I break my Silence, the impact of my Love will be universal and all life in creation will know, feel and receive of it. It will help every individual to break himself free from his bondage in his own way.[34]

Of my own I shall not break my silence; Universal Crisis will make me do so. When the Crisis will reach its absolute culmination, it will make me utter the WORD at that moment.[35]

When I break my Silence the world will be shaken into realization of Who I Am. When I break my Silence the impact will jolt the world out of its spiritual lethargy, and will push open the hearts of all who love Me and are connected with Me.[36]

When I break My Silence it will not be to fill your ears with spiritual lectures. I shall speak only One Word, and this Word will penetrate the hearts of all men and make even the sinner feel that he is meant to be a saint, while the saint shall know that God is in the sinner as much as He is in himself.[37] **When I break my Silence**

my Presence will flood the world, and even an inanimate thing like a stone will feel my Love.[38]

As the results of the release of this Word and the Avatar's spiritual work, Baba predicted a new era of universal brotherhood, peace, compassion, and love of God. Certain other predictions and unresolved questions around Baba's speaking are examined more fully in Chapter 14. Whatever interpretation Baba lovers prefer, the nature of Meher Baba's method as a personal Master remains unchanged.

Challenges to Meher Baba's Claim

Meher Baba's claim of being the Avatar, the Christ, raises profound and skeptical questions. His answers to such reactions shed more light on the nature of the Avatar.

Direct Challenges and Baba's Response

Baba's statements about his divinity were anything but subtle. He knew how most people would react. **When I say I am the Avatar, there are a few who feel happy, some who feel shocked, and many who take me for a hypocrite, a fraud, a supreme egoist, or just mad.**[39]

Some people dismiss Baba as immodest, thinking the Christ would be more "humble" and certainly not so public; but **I am everything . . . and honesty demands that what I am, I must express.**[40] **The greatest greatness and the greatest humility go hand in hand, naturally and without effort. When the Greatest of all says, "I am the Greatest," it is only a spontaneous expression of an infallible truth.**[41]

When Baba was publicly criticized or condemned, his followers were occasionally distressed, but the God-Man **is indifferent to abuse and persecution, for in His true compassion He understands; in His continual experiencing of reality He knows; and in His infinite mercy He forgives.**[42]

I am what I am, whether the world bows down to Me or whether it turns against Me; it does not matter.[43] **No amount of slander can affect or change me, nor any amount of admiration or praise enhance my divinity. Baba is what he is. I was Baba, I am Baba, and I shall forever remain Baba.**[44]

For the purposes of his work, Baba enjoyed opposition and asked his followers to be tolerant: **People who speak ill of me should not be condemned.[45] They should not be hated. They too are unconsciously serving my cause. Just as you are keeping connection with me, so are they often thinking of me.[46]**

Baba was extremely gentle with skeptics in his presence. One questioner asked, "If you are the Christ, why do people not know?" Baba answered, **It is because people cannot know that I have to take this (human) form. Jesus was not known in his time, even by his own intimate and immediate companions. Judas who was all the time near him and kissed him could not understand him. So do you all *not* understand me externally in my physical form; because as the Real, Infinite Christ, I am *within* you, as [I am with]in everybody.[47]**

Another questioner wanted to know whether Baba believed that Jesus was unique among the prophets. **Unique, indeed, from the standpoint of his state and consciousness. The Mahommedans claim that Mahommed is the only prophet. The Buddhists claim Buddha, the Parsis for Zoroaster and the Christians for Christ. Each say that his perfect ideal (of the Prophet) is the unique one. But why bother about that? What do names matter? What is important is the *life* that Jesus lived. *To understand Christ, to know him, one has to live his life. Mere ceremonies and talks, discussions and criticisms don't help one towards knowing Christ.* Christ taught one simple thing, LOVE, and so few of his followers have that love developed![48]**

Meher Baba's Suffering

Some sincere skeptics cannot imagine the Messiah undergoing colds, physical pain, or such mundane disasters as auto accidents, all of which Baba suffered. Baba explained how such things must be: **The Avatar takes on bondage, and therefore (as God-Man) actually "becomes" the role He has assumed and has to really suffer.[49] . . . only the Christ suffers for humanity, although he is the source of all happiness. . . . I suffer as no one could suffer; I suffer because I love.[50]**

I suffer physically and mentally. My physical suffering can be seen. . . . I suffer spiritually because, although in Me I am Free,

in you I see and feel Myself bound by your ignorance; and so I suffer. . . . Why and how can I suffer when I am the Ocean of Power, Knowledge and Bliss? . . .

During His ministry as Avatar, He uses only Infinite Knowledge. He does not make use of His Infinite Power and Infinite Bliss. This is because God incarnates as Man and goes through universal suffering and helplessness in order to emancipate mankind from its ignorance of suffering and helplessness. . . . Such is His Infinite Love and Compassion for His Creation! . . . [Jesus] suffered crucifixion on the cross, but did not help Himself from the Power and Bliss that were His. Instead He cried, "Father, why hast Thou forsaken me!" He said it to Himself, of course, for He was One with God—the Father.[51]

The Question of Miracles

Some might argue that the Avatar should be able to prove his divinity by working miracles. Baba himself chose to avoid performing unnecessary miracles, maintaining that "God has to be known through love." [52]

He gave an illustrative explanation when a new disciple suggested to him that he demonstrate his Godhood to the masses by causing a large building to be erected in a few minutes. Baba declared that no God-realized person would consider doing such a thing: **It would be childish, and its effects would be just the reverse of what you would expect it to be. You think that hundreds of thousands of people would come to me and live spiritual lives. Certainly there would be no limit to the scores of people who would be attracted to me! But almost all of them would be worldly-minded and would ask me to gratify their materialistic desires. Those in need of money would say: "You erected this building in a few minutes, why can't you miraculously produce a few thousand dollars for me?" And even those with the potentialities for a life of renunciation, on hearing of such a miracle would ask me to relieve them from all their troubles, and effect their spiritual salvation at once. . . . This world is an illusion. Therefore, as a rule God-realized persons do not perform great public miracles—which are displays of the Master's power to create further illusion. . . .**[53]

Baba knew he could get allegiance and obedience with spectacular miracles, but he wanted people worshiping the *love* that God has for man, not the *power* that produces miracles. He once explained how people misunderstood him when he was incarnated as Jesus: **When Jesus said, "I and my father are one," he meant that he was God. . . . God created this entire phenomenal universe. That is God's miracle and the miracle of Jesus. . . . Yet it is supposed that Jesus' greatness is that he raised some few dead to life. How ridiculous that is, unless it has some hidden meaning. It is supposed that he is the Saviour because he raised a few dead and gave sight to the blind, creating insignificant illusions in the midst of his great illusion. . . . Had Jesus not raised the dead, had he not performed the miracles, he would not have been crucified, and he wanted to be crucified. He performed the miracles to make certain of being crucified.**[54]

Actually, countless events happened around Baba that would appear miraculous to the Western mind, from a child coming back to life after dying to Baba lovers being saved from certain death when calling on him for help. Baba said he did not do these miracles directly; they were miracles of love for him and the power of his name. Ironically, those who judge spirituality from miraculous phenomena would be overwhelmed by the evidence around him.

Yet he identified himself with miracles of quite another order: **Ages and ages ago I did perform one great miracle, and the whole of this illusion of creation came from me.**[55] **I have said that my miracle will be not to raise the dead but to make one dead to himself to live to God. I have repeatedly said that I will not give sight to the blind, but I will make them blind to the world in order to see God.**[56]

The Call of the Avatar

According to Baba, few accept the Avatar or know of his universal work until long after he has left the physical body. But the primary interest of this volume is the Avatar's secondary role—as a personal Master. Those who would follow him as a personal Master are not entitled to any special dispensation or status; Baba says, **I am for all.** However, potential lovers of the Avatar do have a special new opportunity.

The time is come. I repeat the Call, and bid all come unto me.[57] I have come down from the Highest to your level and if on that level you love me with all your heart, you will come to my level of the Highest, because I am in you.[58]

No matter what vicious qualities one may be possessed of, one should neither hesitate to come to me nor feel any shame in coming before me.[59] Have hope. I have come to help you in surrendering yourselves to the cause of God and accepting his grace of love and truth. I have come to help you in winning the one victory of all victories—to win yourself.[60]

In the next chapter, Baba explains *how* seekers can come to him and follow the path of the Avatar. In Baba's terms, a risk in that direction is a chance well taken.

I am the source of happiness, the Sun of all bliss. But there is a curtain that veils you from the sun and you do not see it. Now, because of your inability to see owing to the curtain, you cannot say there is no sun. The sun is there, shining and spreading its lustre all over the world; but you do not allow its rays to approach you, obstructing them with the veil of ignorance. Remove that and you will see the sun. I will help you to tear open the curtain and enable you to find happiness with it. I love you, I love you all.[61]

I bring the greatest treasure which it is possible for man to receive—a treasure which includes all other treasures, which will endure forever, which increases when shared with others. Be ready to receive it.[62]

CHAPTER 9

Approaching the Avatar

> ***I authoritatively say: I am the Ancient One. I have been saying this to all the world. If you love me with all your heart, then you shall be made free eternally.***
>
> —MEHER BABA, quoted in Purdom, *The God-Man*

According to Meher Baba, the supremely effective use of the aspirant's consciousness is to focus it on a relationship with perfection, with God. Such focusing can be done most easily by concentrating spiritual energy on a Perfect Guide, which reduces the ego, dissolves binding impressions, and gives the Master an open channel for direct assistance in Self-discovery.

Aspirants hoping to follow a Master rarely come across Perfect Masters, who are usually reserved for very advanced souls. And, with one exception, Perfect Masters out of their physical bodies avoid a direct guidance role. That exception is the Avatar, the aspect of God that takes an active interest in the progression of all souls still trapped in limited awareness. The Avatar regularly incarnates in a physical body, clarifies his way, and offers direct assistance to anyone (spiritually advanced or not) who accepts it.

Meher Baba claims to have been the latest advent of God in human form. In or out of his physical body, he invites aspirants to join him. Assuming that Meher Baba is the Avatar of this age, it is important to realize that the way of Meher Baba is essentially the same as the way of Muhammad or Jesus or Buddha or Krishna. To those who are deeply and firmly attached to a previous incarnation of the Avatar, there seems no reason why Baba's message cannot be almost entirely transposed. Esoteric Christians, for example, can take Baba's suggestions as a newly discovered revelation of Jesus. Mystically inclined Jews can feel that their own beloved Messiah is talking directly to them. Muslims drawn to Sufism can listen for undisguised new words of the Prophet. Buddhists on the inner path can eavesdrop on the latest teachings of Gautama. Vedantists or yogis in the Hindu tradition can hear the inspiration of Rama and Krishna re-echo. All those who relate best to a personal manifestation of God may be able to hear their own God speaking to them through the vehicle of Meher Baba.

If the Avataric technique is almost the same for each Avataric incarnation, why the emphasis on Baba? Unless one is deeply attached to another Avataric form, it makes sense to focus on the latest one. His message is least distorted by language, history, and preconception. His energy is the freshest and his guidance is specifically suited to the present culture, civilization, and consciousness.

This chapter centers on the best approach to Meher Baba as the Avatar. The greatest task of the aspirant is to become sensitive to the Avatar's guidance and love by cementing the relationship between human being and Meher Baba, between the limited self and the Real Self. The excerpts found in this chapter are the essence of Meher Baba's method.

Loving Meher Baba

Meher Baba sees the path of love as the most potent. According to Baba, loving God is the greatest love, and loving the Avatar is a timeless technique for loving God. Meher Baba's invitation to seekers, **Love me!** is not a neurotic need for affection. It is an encouragement to pursue fruitfulness on the Avataric path. The following excerpts sketch a clear picture of Baba's priorities for his current and potential lovers.

I am the One who is always lost and found among mankind. It is your love for yourself that loses me and it is your love for me that finds me. Love me above everything.[1] I have not come amongst you for you to bow down to me, to perform my *arti* [song in praise], to worship me. These things are good for the saints, *walis* and

yogis. I expect much more from you. I have come to receive your love from you, and to bestow my love on you. I have descended to your level for the one purpose of bestowing my love on you so that you may love God and become God. The rest is all illusion. Do not expect anything from me except my love for you.[2]

Don't try to understand me. My depth is unfathomable. Just love me.[3] Love me and let God love us. That is what I want. When you love Baba, God will love you, and God's loving means everything.[4]

Saint and sinner, high and low, rich and poor, healthy and sick, man and woman, young and old, beautiful and ugly, are all equal in my eyes. Why? Because I am in everyone. None should hesitate to come to me, meet me and embrace me with love.[5] The only place that can hold Me is the heart. Keep Me close with you—I am always there.[6]

When Baba explained the importance of love for him, he sometimes referred to his previous forms as the Avatar: **Not only in this incarnation but every time I come I stress that love is the remedy.[7]**

What Krishna teaches in the *Gita* goes deep; he does not say anything in a round-about way. He says you can become God. If you love me, follow me; there is no other way.[8] Christ said with divine authority, "Your sins are forgiven;" and I say with divine authority, "Love me and your worries will vanish."[9] Why do we need another prescription? Because humanity would never listen to Him. He said the same thing: "I am the Reality. All follow me. Wake up from the dream!" None listen. The same thing is repeating again. That's why I tell you, love Me more and more and make others love Me. Through your own example, make others happy. God will listen to that.[10]

Baba explained what disciples should ask from the Avatar and what he asks in return: **You say you want God-realization. . . . I want to warn all who approach me that they should not expect health, wealth, wife or children from me. I tell you that those who have associated with me through love have suffered complete material pain. History records this. All I give is God. I want only Love.[11]**

When we love from the bottom of our hearts we give all our good and bad, even our trouble; the lover gives everything and demands nothing in return. Love me like that and Baba is your slave.[12] I am

not your slave. I am the Slave of your Love. Remember that. . . . Nothing can ever be serious except lack of love for Me.[13]

Although I do not perform miracles, I will give anything to whomsoever asks for it from the bottom of the heart. If I am "Baba," everything is possible to me. Ask whole-heartedly and you will get it from me. But this I tell you too, that the one who asks for my love will be the chosen one.[14] **Lose yourself in Baba and you will find that you eternally were Baba.**[15]

From these statements Baba asks for love and yet says paradoxically that the Ocean of Divine Love, the ultimate attainment, is a gift of grace: **I have also said that you cannot love me as I ought to be loved. To do that you must first receive the gift of my love. . . .**[16] The key is receptivity:

It is always infinitely easy for me to give—but it is not always equally easy for you to receive—the gift of my love.[17] **In my inalienable Oneness of Love . . . it is left to you to open your heart and receive love from Me.**[18]

But how does one gain receptivity? The disciple should not worry about the final attainment, but invest in effort and striving: **How very complicated a simple thing has been made! I am giving you a hint—the easiest way to achieve the Goal of life is to leave all and follow me through love. I don't mean that you should leave your house and family. . . . Don't do that! I mean that you be in your house and with your family but love me as I want you to love me—love me above all. That is the simplest way. Another hint—a still more simple way to attain the Goal is to obey Me . . . obey Me implicitly. Is it possible? That is simpler than the simplest thing. Try. If you try, I** [will] **help you.**[19]

Ultimately, Baba reassures all those who think they fail in loving him: **If you cannot love Me, do not worry. I will be loving you.**[20]

Obeying Meher Baba

Although the aspirant should try to love Baba, love cannot be forced. Perfect love for the Avatar cannot be created by an act of will; this fact explains the importance of obedience: **To surrender is higher than to love, and paradoxical as it may seem, to love me as I ought to be loved is impossible, yet to obey me is possible.**[21] Love for Baba involves much more than felt emotion. When the feeling of love is suspended in the aspirant, obedience becomes crucial. Once Baba was asked, "Is it possible to love God merely through obedience when feeling is absent?" Baba replied, **It is the highest form of love.**[22]

Voluntary obedience to the Avatar is a practical attitude that takes the disciple directly to the goal: **Complete remembrance of God, honesty in action, making no one unhappy, being the cause of happiness in others, and no submission to low, selfish, lustful desires, while living a normal worldly life—can lead one to the path of Realization. But complete obedience to the God-Man brings one directly to God.**[23]

Obedience is more important than devotion, even if it is done unwillingly, because gradually, in the process, duality vanishes. When you do what the Master says, the responsibility falls on him, the one you obey, even when you obey unwillingly.[24] **True obedience to one's Master is the greatest and closest of bindings which must inevitably bring in its wake the greatest of all freedoms—the Freedom of the Soul.**[25]

In biographical accounts of Baba's work with individual disciples and lovers, the theme of obedience comes up again and again. Strange or seemingly contradictory orders by Baba would be precisely appropriate even though not understood by his mandali at the time: **I know what has to be done, I know how it is to be done. It is for you to do what I say. Do not be concerned with anything else.**[26] Baba did not demand obedience to test his disciples but to help them safely through the jungles of confusion and karma.

Often, he reminded lovers all over the world about the importance of obedience: **All I ask of you is that you love me most and obey me at all times. Knowing that it is impossible for you to obey me as you should, I help you to carry out wholeheartedly what I give you to do by repeatedly bringing to you the importance of obedience.**[27]

Unquestioning obedience to me, without consciously knowing me, will bring you nearest to me. But it is impossible to obey me literally and spontaneously. If I were in your place, I myself would not be able to do that.[28]

Even though very difficult, voluntary obedience is enhanced by the existence of doubt. **The best thing for you would be to obey me**

cheerfully. In any case, though, to obey me now when you have not yet consciously experienced my greatness is in itself a great thing. Much of the value of obedience is lost once conviction is transformed into actual, conscious knowledge of my reality.[29] Obey instantly. Try even if you cannot. It is not disobedience if you cannot, but you must try. Do not say, "I cannot." Say, "I'll try."[30]

Obedience Reconsidered

The question of obedience to Meher Baba became more subtle after he left his physical body. The value of individualized advice from Baba is clear; he knew infinitely well exactly what experiences lovers needed in order to progress most quickly. He knew precisely how to expose weaknesses and nurture strengths. Obedience gave the Master-surgeon the best opportunity to cut out the ego.

Most Baba lovers who received specific instructions from Baba before January 1969 feel those orders are still applicable. But how can new followers obey him without being sure of his special wishes for them? One source of guidance is found in Baba's comprehensive written and recorded messages. By submerging themselves in this material, new disciples can obtain a basic grounding in Baba's general wishes for his lovers. Then aspirants can apply the general spiritual principles to specific situations in their lives.

A second, perhaps more important approach to obedience involves the faculty of intuition, the voice of enlightened conscience. Intuition for obedience is stimulated by such questions as What would most please Baba in this situation? and How would Baba wish me to act? Cultivating an inner sense demands maximum sincerity and self-honesty. Aspirants should not expect Baba to provide direction by audible voices or external signs. More likely, he will respond through one's own intuition and discrimination, almost as an inner gyroscope. Actually, Baba set a precedent for new seekers in the last few years of his physical life. He began to answer questions from his lovers in very general ways, telling them to do what they felt in their hearts, and stressing that he would be with them in their decision-making process.

Assuming the aspirant is sincere, a trial-and-error process can mature his ability to intuit the specific guidance Baba might give if he were physically present: **Neither praise nor blame should distract**

you from the path of your duty. Leave aside all other considerations; if your conscience tells you that you have discharged the duty properly, that is enough. Your conscience is the best judge. It is human to err, and there must be mistakes, you can only do your best.[31] As summarized by one of Baba's close mandali, "When you read Baba's literature, when you read his discourses, you understand what type of life Baba would like you to lead. So you lead that type of life; satisfy your conscience also. That is the best form of obeying."[32]

Surrendering to Meher Baba

Another dimension of the Avataric path involves surrender. In one sense surrender is the culmination of loving and obeying the Master: **Love is a gift from God to man, obedience is a gift from master to man, and surrender is a gift from man to master. The one who loves, desires to do the will of the beloved, and seeks union with the beloved. Obedience performs the will of the beloved and seeks the pleasure of the beloved. Surrender resigns to the will of the beloved and seeks nothing.**[33] **The easiest and safest way to lose one's finite ego is by completely surrendering to the Perfect Master. . . . Such complete surrenderance to the Perfect Master is, in itself, Freedom.**[34]

A unique surrender to the Master occurs when **the lover surrenders completely to Christ, to the *Avatar*, to the God-Man. He lives, not for himself, but for the Master. This is the highest type of lover.**[35]

The notion of surrender may be disturbing to seekers who value their independence. However, when an aspirant realizes that true liberation is **surrenderance of the false and the inheritance of the Truth,** surrender becomes consistent with independence and real freedom of choice. "To be a disciple of a Perfect One never involves the surrender of the right to think and feel and act by oneself. It does not mean ceasing to be true to the inner voice of the Highest Self within. On the contrary, discipleship of a Perfect One facilitates the pursuit of that Higher Self."[36]

Understandably, Meher Baba invited his lovers to try to surrender to him: **If you seek to live perpetually, then crave for the**

death of your "deceptive self" at the hands of "Complete Surrender" to me. This Yoga is the Essence of all yogas in one. . . . To realize this Truth of Unchangeable, Indivisible, All-pervading Existence, the simplest way is to surrender to Me *completely;* so completely that you are not even conscious of your surrender. . . .[37] Completely surrender yourselves to me so that my wish becomes your law and my love sustains your being. . . . He who succeeds, ultimately not only finds me, but becomes me and realises the aim of life.[38]

To his lovers, Baba suggested ways of practicing surrender: **I want you all to listen very carefully to what I say. It appears so simple, yet it is so very important for My lovers. To love Me is to lose yourself in Me and to find Me as your own Self is to leave all your pleasures and pains to Me.[39] Be resigned completely to my Will and my Will will be yours.[40] If you do wrong, think Baba is doing wrong. If you get a pain, think it is Baba having a pain. If you do all this sincerely, you will know something and forget yourself and do all for Baba.[41]**

There are three interrelated elements in the aspirant's attempted surrender to Meher Baba. The first includes a resignation to everything as Baba's will. Such resignation does not imply passivity or apathy—Baba usually encouraged enthusiastic energy in worldly duties. It means being able to leave the *results* of one's best efforts to Baba, trying not to get ego-involved in success or failure. It also includes trust in Baba, a confidence that all events, positive or negative, can be helpful for spiritual growth: **I want you to remain undisturbed and unshaken by the force of life's currents, for whatever the circumstances, they too will be of my own creation. If you endure your lot with patience and contentment, accepting it as His will, you are loving God.[42]**

A second facet of the process of surrender involves making Baba the nucleus of one's activities, creating a "provisional ego"—adopting the attitude of doing things for Baba, not for oneself. The objective is not to enhance the ego, but to give it up: **Seek me not to extricate you from your predicaments, but find me to surrender yourself wholeheartedly to my Will. . . . Do not ask me to bless you with a good job, but desire to serve me more diligently and honestly without expectation of reward. Never beg of me to save your life or the lives of your dear ones, but beg of me to accept you**

and permit you to lay down your life for me. Never expect me to cure you of your bodily afflictions, but beseech me to cure you of your ignorance.[43]

A third aspect involves realizing the near impossibility of total and complete surrender to Baba while *aspiring* to surrender, starting to build the creative habit of resignation, fostering internal dependence on Baba as one's real Self. Surrendering to the Avatar has always been a private, internal process. It need not be affected by Meher Baba's physical passing.

Taken together, the trinity of love, obedience, and surrender forms a basic unity on the path of the God-Man: **One who loves, is the lover of the beloved. One who obeys is the beloved of the beloved. One who surrenders all—body, mind and all else—has no existence other than that of the beloved, who alone exists in him. Therefore greater than love is obedience, and greater than obedience is surrender. And yet, as words, all three can be summed up in one phrase—love-divine.**[44]

Holding On to Meher Baba's *Daaman*

Baba used a concept that nicely integrates the essence of following him on the path of the God-Man: holding fast to the *daaman.* Literally, *daaman* means the hem of a garment such as a robe or skirt. Applied to the spiritual path, the image represents the disciple holding on to the Master. As Baba uses the phrase, holding on to his *daaman* includes a deep orientation of love, obedience, and surrender, with a special emphasis on faith and commitment.

The aim of life is to love God. The goal of life is to become one with God. The surest and quickest way to achieve this goal is to hold on to my daaman by loving me more and more.[45] **Understanding has no meaning. Love has meaning. Obedience has more meaning. Holding my *daaman* has most meaning.**[46]

Baba urged his lovers to stick to him with the same intensity with which a blind mountain climber would hang on to an experienced guide: **So long as you keep your grip tight it matters little whether you are a saint or sinner. . . . To stick to me means to keep me pleased at the cost of your own comforts and pleasures. It means to remain resigned to my will whether you keep good health or bad,**

whether you make money or lose it, and whether you gain name and fame or become the laughingstock of others.[47]

Many spiritual teachers promise instant bliss. Not so the Avataric path; but holding on to the *daaman* is well worth the effort for Baba's lovers: **There is no *shanti*** [peace of mind] **on this Path. If you want peace of mind, then you can get it elsewhere, and in other ways. You can go for nice long walks or listen to soothing music or take sedatives or go to Saints and Sadhus. But here is not the place to come for it; for if you come to Me, remember that the spiritual Path is full of hardships and sufferings. . . .**[48]

But if you want to see God and to become one with God, then the only solution is to catch hold of my *daaman*. If you care only for God, and if you have the one sole sincere desire for union [God-realization], **then hold on to my *daaman* exclusively.**[49] **If you obey me and hold on to my *daaman*, where I am you will be.**[50]

Of course, holding on to the *daaman* is most relevant after an aspirant's initial relationship with Baba becomes intensified. But Baba predicted that even dedicated lovers would have their sticking power severely tested. Then, hanging on becomes critical: **Hold fast to Me so that I will take you where I go, otherwise you will be lost. I am the Emperor. If you belong to Me, you will have access to the Infinite Treasure that is Mine.**[51]

Realizing Meher Baba

Readers who may still be put off or confused by Baba's wishes for total surrender and commitment to him should recall the underlying mystical foundation of his statements. Meher Baba's invitation to tread the Avataric path comes from God as infinite consciousness. Following Meher Baba is nothing other than following God. Following Baba as God is following one's real Self. Realizing God mystically involves the true experience of one's real identity. Baba made this last fact especially clear when he promised his lovers that he would reveal himself as he "really is" at the end of their spiritual journey:

Once in a while God takes birth because of His Love for His creation. I am born in human form so that you may see me as you are, and if you are fortunate to know me and love me then some

day you will see me as I really am.[52] I am the Divine Beloved worthy of being loved because I am Love. He who loves me because of this will be blessed with unlimited sight and will see me as I am.[53] Then as soon as you see me as I really am, you will find yourself to be your own infinite and eternal self.[54] No sooner do you get that Experience than you feel liberated and experience infinite bliss.[55]

In the deepest sense Meher Baba's prescription for spiritual advancement is none other than every aspirant's real inner voice speaking with absolute clarity and authority. Many seekers report an uncanny familiarity when first exposed to Baba's writings, as if they had somehow already known the truth of his statements. It is almost as if the aspirant were speaking to himself, which, perhaps, he is.

The Process of Realization

Realization may be seen as the ultimate discovery of the soul. It is a finding of Reality, an experience of what is always there. To follow God as the Avatar to the end of the spiritual journey is to find him, to know him, to love him, to become him, and finally, to realize him. For those who are determined to find him, Baba once set forth twelve ways of realization:

1. LONGING. If you experience that same longing and thirst for union with me as one who has been lying for days in the hot sun of the Sahara experiences the longing for water, then you will realise me.

2. PEACE OF MIND. If you have the peace of a frozen lake, then too you will realise me.

3. HUMILITY. If you have the humility of the earth which can be moulded into any shape, then you will know me.

4. DESPERATION. If you experience the desperation that causes a man to commit suicide and you feel that you cannot live without seeing me, then you will see me.

5. FAITH. If you have the complete faith that Kalyan had for his Master, in believing it was night although it was day (because his Master said so), then you will know me.

6. FIDELITY. If you have the fidelity that the breath has in giving you company, even without your constantly feeling it, till

the end of your life (that both in happiness and suffering gives you company and never turns against you), then you will know me.

7. CONTROL THROUGH LOVE. When your love for me drives away your lust for the things of the senses, then you realise me.

8. SELFLESS SERVICE. If you have the quality of selfless service unaffected by results, similar to that of the sun which serves the world by shining on all creation—on the grass in the field, on the birds in the air, on the beasts in the forest—on all mankind with its sinner and its saint, its rich and its poor, unconscious of their attitude towards it, then you will win me.

9. RENUNCIATION. If you renounce for me everything physical, mental and spiritual, then you have me.

10. OBEDIENCE. If your obedience is as spontaneous, complete and natural as the light is to the eye or the smell to the nose, then you come to me.

11. SURRENDERANCE. If your surrenderance to me is as whole-hearted as that of one who, suffering from insomnia, surrenders to sudden sleep without fear of being lost, then you have me.

12. LOVE. If you have that love for me which St. Francis had for Jesus, then not only will you realise me but you will please me.[56]

He who succeeds ultimately not only finds me but becomes me and realizes the aim of life.[57]

CHAPTER 10

Following the Way of Meher Baba

> ***Serve others with the understanding that in them you are serving Me. Be resigned completely to My will and My will will be yours. Let nothing shake your faith in Me and all your bindings will be shaken off.***
>
> —MEHER BABA, *The Awakener*

Meher Baba has described the essential requirements of approaching him as the Avatar. The full mastery of the method of love, obedience, surrender, and commitment is both simple and nearly impossible.

If Meher Baba was explicit about the major strategies on the Avataric path, he was equally direct about the minor tactics. It is comforting to know that the Avatar understands the plight of the average aspirant even while outlining the criteria for perfect discipleship. Of course, for those few souls completely smitten with love and faith for the Avatar, the question of practical application is almost irrelevant. Their lives *are* the embodiment of the method. However, the vast majority who explore Baba's path must pursue it with conscious determination. Meher Baba spent considerable effort explaining how aspirants might integrate their spiritual development with the practical demands of ordinary life. In the pages following, Baba illustrates the implications of his method for attitudes and behavior in the world.

The Practice of Discipleship

The working relationship between an aspirant and Meher Baba as one's Master can be called discipleship. This unique relationship requires the seeker's acceptance: **When an aspirant becomes voluntarily affiliated with a Master, he is said to have become a disciple. But if this affiliation is merely formal, it does not constitute true discipleship. The relationship between disciple and Master is utterly different from the legal relations which create rights and liabilities through verbal transactions or formal agreements. Discipleship is one of the fundamental features which characterise the life of the advanced aspirant, and it does not come into existence through any artificial procedure. . . . It is primarily a relation between the lover and his Divine Beloved. From the spiritual point of view it is the most important relationship into which a person can enter.**[1]

Suppose an aspirant has made the first commitment to attempt Meher Baba's path. In most spiritual movements, discipleship is marked by certain religious practices, activities, or rules. Although Baba's method is remarkably free of structured rules or activities, he explained the comparative value of various practices.

Ceremonial Practices and Prayer

The messages of history's great spiritual figures tend to become obscured by the very religions built around them. Baba cautioned his disciples about the danger of burying the truth under dogma, ritual, and ceremony: **For most persons, the outer ceremonies and rituals prevalent in the diverse religions are the established approach to God and Divinity. They are regarded as indispensable. However, they are neither essential nor necessary, though at times they have been allowed or given by masters by way of inevitable accommodation to human weakness. They may also be practiced with benefit when they are thus allowed or given by a master, but only during the period for which they have been prescribed, and in the context in which they are intended to be given effect.**[2]

Rituals and ceremonies cannot carry one very far towards the path, and if they are unintelligently followed they bind as much as any other unintelligent action. In fact, when they are deprived of all inner life they are in a sense more dangerous than other unintelligent action, because they are pursued in the belief that they help towards God-realization. Due to this element of self-delusion, lifeless forms and ceremonies become a sidetrack to the path.

Through mere force of habit one can become so attached to these external forms that intense suffering may be required to dispel their imaginary value.[3]

Baba insisted that his path should be kept free of dependence on any external forms of worship: **To clothe worship with the garments of ceremony and ritual is to expose Me to the cold winds of ignorance. Tear the curtain of set ceremonies and rituals and you will find that I am the Worshipped, the Worship and the Worshipper. To faithfully love God-Man is to truly worship God.**[4]

Prayer from the heart, however, can, according to Baba, be an exquisite devotional act. **What constitutes the essence of prayer? Many prayers to God are current among the lovers of God, arising as they do from diverse cultural contexts. Some of the prayers invariably contain an element of asking something from God, either material or spiritual. In fact, God is so merciful and bountiful that even without their asking He always gives much more than His lovers can receive. He knows their real needs more deeply than they do. Therefore the element of asking something from God is superfluous. It often mars the inner love and worship which a prayer tries to express.**[5]

The prayer God hears is the prayer of the heart; that raising of the heart, that suffering of the heart, that is what God pays attention to.[6] **The ideal prayer to the Lord is nothing more than spontaneous praise of His being. You praise Him, not in the spirit of bargain but in the spirit of self-forgetful appreciation of what He really is. . . . In the entire spiritual panorama of the universe nothing is more sublime than a spontaneous prayer. It gushes out of the human heart, filled with appreciative joy. . . . It is a return to one's own being.**[7]

Baba gave two formal prayers that could be recited by his disciples if they wished. The "Master's Prayer" is a prayer in praise of God. The "Prayer of Repentance" is intended as a prayer of the heart. On special occasions, Baba would have these prayers read by his lovers. Both are found in Appendix A.

The Disciple and His Body

Some are surprised to learn that Baba emphasized no particular regimen, diet, fasting, or other kind of physical austerity. He asked his disciples only to use common sense and discrimination, to neither pamper their bodies nor be careless with them.

In 1927 Baba asked his mandali which was the largest jail in India. Some thought Ahmednagar, others Poona, others Bombay, others guessed elsewhere. Baba smiled and said the largest jail on earth was their bodies.[8] In a more formal discourse, Baba advised nonattachment to the body:

The physical body cannot exist without food, and therefore in an indirect sense they are one and the same. The body assimilates that portion of the food which is useful for its maintenance, and throws out that portion which is useless. That which is discarded is as much part of the food that was consumed as that which is assimilated. If man is so supremely indifferent to the eliminated refuse, why should he not feel the same detachment towards the assimilated food which, for practical purposes, becomes his body? Why should he shed tears when, after death, the body itself is cast off to the care of earthworms or to consuming flames?[9]

Baba encouraged his lovers to eat well but without faddism. Once, overhearing some Indian devotees who were pridefully championing vegetarianism, Baba reminded them that what came *out* of their mouth was much more important than what went *into* it. Overall, Baba advised, **Take good care of your body, but do not be a slave to it. If you think constantly of its welfare, you are like the miser who thinks constantly of his gold.**[10]

Faith and the Disciple

From Baba's viewpoint, mere *belief* in God is not the key to spiritual development: **Some who have faith and believe in God lead a life without character and fail to make any spiritual progress, while there are others who do not even believe in God but lead such a noble life that they automatically come closer to God.**[11] True *faith* is something different, and Baba sees no conflict between it and the faculty of reason.

True faith is grounded in the deeper experiences of the spirit and the unerring deliverances of purified intuition. It is not to be regarded as the antithesis of critical reason but as the unfailing guide of critical reason. . . . This does not mean, however, that

faith need at any stage be blind, in the sense that it is not allowed to be examined by critical intellect. True faith is a form of sight and not of blindness. It need not be afraid of the free functioning of critical reason.[12] **Unless you question you will never learn.**[13]

For the successful disciple, faith in Meher Baba is immensely helpful, but not at thc expense of self-confidence. Different from egoistic pride, true self-confidence leads naturally to faith in the Master. **If a man has no faith in himself, he cannot develop those qualities which invite and foster faith from others. The confidence that you can remain loyal under all sorts of trying circumstances to your own perception of the best, is the very foundation of the superstructure of a reliable character.**[14]

The key to real faith in oneself is faith in the Master, which **becomes all-important because it nourishes and sustains faith in oneself and faith in life in the very teeth of setbacks and failures, handicaps and difficulties, limitations and failings.**[15] **The self-confidence which is thus in perpetual danger of being shattered, can be securely established only when the man has before him the vision of the living example of perfection, and has faith in it.**[16] **In the Master, man sees his own ideal realised; the Master is what his own deeper self would rather be. He sees in the Master the reflection of the best in himself which is yet to be, but which he will surely one day attain. Faith in the Master therefore becomes the chief motive-power for realising the divinity which is latent in man.**[17]

Faith in Meher Baba is most crucial after a lover has become a committed disciple. **The right of testing the Master through critical reasoning has always been conceded to the disciples; but if, after testing and being satisfied about the perfection of the Master, the disciple shows any wavering of faith, it is a result of a deplorable deficiency in his sincerity of approach and integrity of purpose.**[18]

Faith in Meher Baba

Baba urged his lovers to nurture faith in him and his divinity, but not at the expense of honesty: **Do not propagate what you do not feel. What your heart says and what your conscience dictates about me, pour out without hesitation. Be unmindful of whether you are ridiculed or accepted in pouring out your heart for me, or against me, to others.**

If you take Baba as God, say so; do not hesitate. If you think Baba is the Devil, say it. Do not be afraid. I am everything that you take me to be, and I am also beyond everything. If your conscience says that Baba is the Avatar, say it even if you are stoned for it. But if you feel that he is not, then say that you feel that Baba is not the Avatar.[19]

The sincere newcomer may find it difficult to generate instant belief in Baba, but that is no real barrier. Once a daughter of a clergyman met Baba and admitted that she did not believe in him. And yet she wished she could share that faith which others had for him. Baba responded, **But why? . . . Since what you really want is *within* yourself, you will find it only there. My part is to help you find it, whether you believe in me or not. I will help you even if you don't want my help. When the sun is high in the heavens you feel its warmth, whether you wish to or not.**[20]

There comes a point, however, when the aspirant does best by making a clear decision about Baba and then sticking to it. **If all of you are convinced that Baba is the Avatar, God Incarnate, the question of confusion does not arise at all. In this case, just hold fast to my *daaman* and close all doors for confusion and conflict to enter your minds. If you are not convinced, leave me. Seek someone else. But if you try to stick to me with a wavering mind, without being convinced of my divinity, you will be just like a nut caught in the crusher.**[21]

Aspiring Baba disciples may go through long periods of doubt and struggle with their intuition. But once the aspirants finally choose to continue on the Avataric path, Baba urges them to foster maximum faith: **All my actions are my divine response born of My divine love. . . . Therefore uproot all doubt and remember well that whatever I do is for the best.**[22]

A post, to stand erect and firm, must have its butt-end sunk well into the ground. Likewise, my lover needs to have the base of his faith deeply embedded in my Divinity if he would remain steadfast in his love.[23] **So I say with divine authority, approach me with unfailing faith, love and devotion, and with the longing to receive my Divine Love and Grace.**[24]

As put by one of Baba's long-time mandali, "Avatar Meher Baba has given to His true lovers . . . two things which do not change and will not change. . . . The first . . . that 'God is' and the second, that 'Meher Baba is God.' . . . one who gets the Light of

Knowledge is really great because he sees everything; but for one to have an unchanging certainty of the existence of Meher Baba as God in the darkness of ignorance is in a way greater as a gift of God. Meher Baba alone could give it." [25]

Qualifications of the Successful Disciple

The aspirant who has made an internal commitment to Baba and then strives to follow Baba's path is confronted with the difficulty of integrating the deepest mysteries of the inner life with the practicalities of an imperfect personality in an imperfect society. Helpfully, Baba pointed to certain qualities that lead not only to harmonious living but also to spiritual growth.

Persistence and Forbearance

Once a man is determined to realize the Truth he finds that his path is beset with many difficulties, and there are very few who persist with steady courage till the very end. It is easy to give up effort when one is confronted with obstacles.[26]

The need for persistence may be especially keen after the aspirant has pursued the path for a while. Once, seeing the dejection of some disciples, Baba explained: **One generally passes through three stages in the spiritual life. The first is burning enthusiasm, when the aspirant is imbued with the keen desire of seeing and experiencing the unknown. The second is disappointment, the third divine bliss. The second stage, in which you are at present, is very long. Since you cannot escape from it or remedy it, you must put up with it cheerfully. Don't leave me in any case.**[27]

A Baba lover must be able to endure the pressures of a world that is **addicted to false values.** He must **develop that quality which would enable him to face and accept the world as it is. . . .**

As the aspirant advances on the Path he acquires, through his contact with the Master, an increasingly deeper understanding of true love. This makes him painfully sensitive to those impacts from outside which not only do not taste of love, but actually bring him into contact with cold contempt, cynical callousness, agonizing apathy and unabating hatred. All these impacts try his forbearance

to the utmost. . . . The task of forbearance would be easy if the aspirant could become reconciled to the ways of the world and accept them without challenge. Having seen the higher, however, it becomes his imperative duty to stand by it, even if the whole world opposes him. Loyalty to the higher truth of his own perception demands unshakable moral courage and readiness to face the criticism, scorn and even hatred of those who have not yet begun to open out to the truth. . . . To love the world and serve it in the ways of the Masters is no game for the weak and faint-hearted.[28]

Often such forbearance involves reacting to others. **No matter how harshly the opposing party treats you, always be calm. Always, however much you are found fault with or are blamed or have high words said to you, bear all with patience. This is real bravery and courage.[29]**

Yet, **There lies the fun of the game, to meet opposition, to face and encounter it. If not, life becomes dull and monotonous. One can find spirituality only through opposition.[30]**

Fighting Worry

Among the many things which the aspirant needs to cultivate there are few which are as important as cheerfulness, enthusiasm and equipoise, and these are rendered impossible unless he succeeds in cutting out worry from his life. When the mind is gloomy, depressed or disturbed its action is chaotic and binding.[31] One must try to be cheerful even in trying periods.[32] It is a divine art to look cheerful. It helps others.[33]

The easy way is not to make much of things. Take them lightly. Say to yourself, "I am meant to be happy, to make others happy." . . . Don't suggest to your mind, "I am tired, haggard, depressed." That will make you feel worse.[34]

Meher Baba's considerable emphasis on the avoidance of worry is a strong spiritual hint. **Don't worry. Worry accumulates and grows in strength, becomes a habit long after the original cause has ceased to be. . . . When you were young, this and that happened, you cried, you felt sad, and worry began, and after fifty years you still worry, although the time when worry began in you has gone. If another fifty years passes you could at the end of that time be still worrying about something which was happening now. It is crazy.[35]**

Baba asked one devotee, **Will you promise Me one thing? You say you love Me. You say you want to please Me and to see Me happy. Then remember, be happy and do not worry. I will help you. I know all. I know how deep is your love. Just do as I say. Love Me and leave the rest to Me.**[36]

On other occasions, Baba reassured his followers that their worries would vanish into insignificance when he broke his Silence and manifested. **All that frightens and confuses you and grips you with despair is your own shadow. When the Sun of Love manifests in Its Glory, and all faces are turned towards that Radiance, all shadows will have disappeared—even the memory of them will have vanished. . . . Be composed in the Reality of My Love, for all confusion and despair is your own shadow which will vanish when I speak The Word.**[37]

Attitude toward Suffering

As Baba once remarked, **Real happiness lies in Oneness; wherever there is duality, there is trouble.**[38] Because human beings live in duality, they suffer. Baba's priority is to lead his lovers to permanent happiness, not temporary pleasure. Obviously, the aspirant should avoid self-imposed suffering, but an enlightened attitude can transmute unavoidable suffering into spiritual advantage.

Not all suffering is bad. When suffering leads to the eternal happiness of desirelessness, it should be regarded as a blessing in disguise.[39] **People should look upon physical and mental suffering as gifts from God. They bring their own lessons of the futility of the passing, and of the intrinsic worth of the eternal.**[40] **The degrees of the tasting of bliss vary in accordance with the proportionate experience of suffering.**[41] **The real happiness which comes through realizing God is worth all the physical and mental suffering in the universe. Then all suffering is as if it had never been.**[42]

Do not get disheartened or alarmed when adversity, calamity or misfortunes pour upon you. Thank God, for He has thereby given you the opportunity of acquiring forbearance and fortitude. One who has acquired the power of bearing with adversity can easily enter upon the spiritual Path.[43]

Man or woman, rich or poor, great or small—each is under the spell of some sort of suffering. The relief from every kind of suffer-

ing is within ourselves if we try, under all circumstances and in every walk of life, to think honestly, to act honestly, and to live honestly. When we put out wholehearted faith in God, that relief will be found.[44]

Meher Baba's Work on the Ego

Meher Baba works as an *active* Master, an inner force who stimulates and guides spiritual development. Along with increased joy and inspiration, Baba lovers may encounter more "trouble" after becoming established on Baba's path. If self-satisfied, peaceful stagnation is highly valued, involvement with Meher Baba is downright dangerous. The reason is simple: Baba's task is to assist in the elimination of the ego. Baba as the inner Master may precipitate internal crises, bring weaknesses to the surface, and force self-confrontation at a rate and level that can leave his lovers breathless. Yet they have the opportunity of becoming wiser in just those personal areas most ripe for rapid spiritual growth.

In the same way that Baba provides solace and spiritual uplift when disciples are depressed or desperate, he may stir up inferiority feelings in lovers falling prey to pride. Indeed, aspirants committed to Baba find situations arising that pound away at their spiritual weaknesses in an uncannily appropriate way. Although he promised never to push his lovers beyond their point of tolerance, Baba reminded a close woman disciple who was hurt by the cruelty of another:

Remember, in the future, that when anyone hurts you, it is I who hurt you; when anyone loves you, it is I who loves you; when anyone laughs at you, it is I who am laughing; when you love anyone it is I whom you love. I am in all things. How can you realize my Infinite Presence if you shrink from me in those who hurt you and welcome me only in those who please you?[45]

At times, Baba may allow an aspirant to feel his loving presence; at other times, the disciple may feel a vacuum. As Baba said about his working, **I push you away, then I draw you close; again I push you off and draw you even closer. . . .**[46]

Such a process helps the disciple accomplish in one lifetime that which might take hundreds in the ordinary course of evolution. Because the Avatar has access to the disciple's past history, he knows the disciple's most urgent spiritual tasks and initiates pertinent internal crises, while providing the inspiration and love to handle them creatively.

On Meher Baba's path, spiritual growth sprints forth in the midst of ordinary life. To facilitate this growth, the aspiring Baba lover must try to perfect his character as well as his relationship to every living thing and every role offered by the law of karma. To follow Meher Baba, it matters not where the disciple is located or what constitutes his duties to people and society. The practical application of Baba's method is constant and universal; one can always try to fulfill the wishes of the inner Master.

It is but for the very few to annihilate their very existence and merge in me. To those others who want to love me, I have given points for them to follow. Love means "Love." It has no superficiality or formalities. The lover has to keep the wish of the Beloved and has to keep the Beloved always pleased and happy. What are the wishes of your Beloved—if you take me to be your Beloved? Here they are:

(1) Do not shirk your responsibilities—such as home, family, office, jobs, etc.

(2) Attend faithfully to your worldly duties, but keep at the back of your mind that all this is Baba's.

(3) When you feel happy, think: "Baba wants me to be happy." When you suffer, think: "Baba wants me to suffer."

(4) Be resigned to every situation and think honestly and sincerely: "Baba has placed me in this situation."

(5) With the understanding that Baba is in everyone, try to help and serve others.[47]

CHAPTER 11

Remembrance

The best course for My lover is to remember Me wholeheartedly as much as he can, and to remain happy. So try to love Me by remembering Me, and leave the rest to Me.
—MEHER BABA, *Darshan Hours*

This is intended to be a *practical* book, so that readers interested in Baba will know what to *do* and how best to proceed on his path. The preceding chapters have given a condensed introduction to the life, thought, and general methods of Meher Baba, but some readers might desire other techniques for perfecting the attributes of successful discipleship.

Remembrance is a simple, concrete, and conscious technique. Remembrance of Meher Baba is especially useful for the aspirant who wishes to cultivate creative spiritual activity *at any moment, at any place, in any situation*. Remembrance consists simply of *remembering Meher Baba*, thinking of him as much as possible: his name, his words, his image, his love, and so forth. Remembrance is related intimately with love, obedience, and spiritual integration.

Remembrance as a Method

The spiritual advantage of remembrance is both its simplicity and its efficacy in transforming consciousness.

Identification with Perfection

Baba states that consciousness tends to identify and merge with the contents of awareness. An aspirant picks up mental impressions of qualities associated with the objects of thought. So the more consciousness thinks of perfection, the more perfect it tends to become. When the focus is amplified by strong positive emotion, the influence on consciousness is even more powerful. **By meditation on a Perfect Master who is divine and fully conscious of his divinity, the individual who is divine but not fully conscious of his divinity is led into Divine Self-Consciousness.[1] In thinking day and night of the Master, the disciple *nearly* achieves the ultimate objective which is the aim of the diverse practices of meditation and concentration.[2]**

Just as a man who admires the character of Napoleon and constantly thinks about him has a tendency to become like him, so an aspirant who admires some spiritually perfect person and constantly thinks about him has a tendency to become spiritually perfect. A suitable object for personal meditation is a living Master or Avatar or Masters and Avatars of the past. It is important that the object of meditation be spiritually perfect. If the person selected for meditation happens to be spiritually imperfect, there is every chance of his frailties percolating into the mind of the aspirant who meditates upon him. . . .

Personal meditation often begins with the admiration which an aspirant feels spontaneously for some divine quality which he sees in the Master. By allowing the mind to dwell upon the divine qualities expressed in the life of the Master, the aspirant imbibes them into his own being.[3]

Once, Baba told some disciples, **If those who love me will just for one minute be silent in their minds just before they go to bed and think of me and picture me in the silence of their minds, and do that regularly, this veil of ignorance will disappear and this bliss that I speak of and which all long for will be experienced.[4]**

Direct Effect on Sanskaras

As Baba has explained, one of the great obstructions to full awareness is the limiting effect of *sanskaras.* It is almost impossible to block out undesirable impressions, but they can be neutralized by impressions of perfection. Remembrance of God, specifically of Meher Baba, can reduce the impact of undesirable impressions and keep them from being translated into action. Remembrance of Baba serves as insulation against the grip of illusion.

What is fasting the mind? It is having no thoughts. But this is impossible. But when you entrust your mind to me by constantly remembering me, there are no thoughts left on which the mind can feed.[5] The fire of divine love alone can destroy all impressions once and for all. However, remembering me can keep down the impurities in the impressions in your mind.[6]

Direct Effect on the Ego

A third advantage of remembrance involves that integrated set of impressions called the ego. Baba suggests that love and surrenderance to the Master diminishes preoccupation with the limiting ego and that the aspirant should develop a provisional ego. Remembering Baba can fortify the provisional ego.

Think always of me, whatever you may be doing; then gradually you will realize that it is I doing everything through you.[7] The less you think of yourself and the more you think of Baba, the sooner the ego goes and Baba remains. When you—"ego"—go away entirely, I am one with you. So bit by bit, you have to go. . . . So better think of me when you eat, sleep, see or hear. Enjoy all, don't discard anything, but think it is Baba—Baba who enjoys, Baba who is eating. It is Baba sleeping soundly and when you wake up, remember it is Baba getting up! Keep this one thought constantly with you.[8]

If you dance for me, you do as much good as one who meditates on me. Some like work, some like play, but when you do it for me, then it is the same. . . . Try to forget yourself and do all for Baba. Let it be Baba all the time![9]

A reasonable aspirant might ask how Baba can be remembered in the midst of intense activity. Baba illustrated how with a story. **Hazrat Nizamuddin Awliya, the Perfect Master of Delhi, was once asked by a visitor how one should live in the world. At that moment it so happened that a few women were passing by with pitchers of water balanced on their heads, and, as they walked, they gossiped and gesticulated. Pointing to them Nizamuddin said, "Look at those women—*that's* how you should live in the world." Asked to**

explain this cryptic remark, the Master continued, "These women returning from the well with pitchers balanced on their heads seem to be thinking of nothing else but exchanging tid-bits of gossip with each other; and yet they are all the time concentrating on something far more important, on balancing the pitchers on their heads. Thus, whatever your body, your senses or the purely surface part of your mind may be occupied with, see that the root of your mind is constantly focused on God!"[10]

Thus, Baba reminded his lovers, **The best is just to remember Me and forget everything else, leave everything to Me. . . . Try to remember me, try to please me, try to do as I wish. That is how you should live in the world; otherwise it is too complicated.[11]**

Reminder of Appropriate Activity

Remembrance can also help the aspirant maintain perspective about life and appreciate his real priorities. Remembering Baba reminds the disciple of spiritually appropriate action: **Therefore when you feel angry or have lustful thoughts, remember Baba at once. . . . In that manner you can prevent unwanted thoughts from turning into unwanted actions, and thus eventually bring your heart to the purification required for me to manifest therein. But it is not child's play to remember me constantly during your moments of excitement. If, in spite of being very angry, you refrain from expressing anger, it is indeed a great achievement.[12]**

Worry, another limiting activity of the mind, is also resolved by remembering Baba. **If at all you must worry, let it be how to remember me constantly. This is worthwhile worry because it will bring about the end of worry. Think of me more and more, and all your worries will disappear into the nothing they really are. My will works out to awaken you to this.[13]**

The probable meaning of Baba's last sentence is illustrated by a message given many years ago to a close Western disciple: **At times you feel 100% miserable. When everything goes wrong the mind becomes helpless and has to rely on the heart. These are the moments when you resign to My will and rely solely on My help. When you leave all to Me, I dare not neglect you and you get relief from your predicament.**

Building a Channel to Baba

Remembrance of Meher Baba intensifies the working relationship between Avatar and disciple. **Anytime a person's thoughts turn truly to me, I am truly with them.**[14] According to Baba, remembrance of the Master establishes a mental contact that deepens the internal relationship.

Such mental contact with the Master is often as fruitful and effective as his physical *darshana.* The inward repetition of such mental contacts is like constructing a channel between Master and aspirant, who becomes thereby the recipient of the grace, love and light which are constantly flowing from the Master in spite of the apparent distance between them. Thus, the help of the Master goes out not only to those who happen to be in his physical presence but also to others who establish mental contact with him.[15]

Often Baba made the point that physical proximity to him was unnecessary. It follows that mental contact through remembrance is equally possible after his release from the body. Baba pointed out that the presence of the Avatar is always there. Remembrance helps the aspirant *know* it: . . . **I like being meditated upon because then I help directly.**[16] **Think of Me to such an extent that you see Me, however far away I may be.**[17]

Service to Others

An unexpected benefit of remembrance is its helpfulness to others. Because the Avatar uses the love and energy directed toward him, remembering Meher Baba with love becomes a significant service to humanity.

The unity and solidarity of the inner plane makes it possible for the Master to use his disciple as a medium for his work even when the disciple is unconscious of serving this larger purpose of the Master. This is possible because the disciple, through his love and understanding of the Master as well as his obedience and surrender, establishes a rapport with the Master and comes into tune with him. . . . The Master feeds upon the love of his disciples and utilises the spiritual forces released by them for his universal work. In this way the Master is like the relaying station which receives a

song only in order to broadcast it to the world at large. To love the Master is to love all, not merely symbolically but actually; for what the Master receives on the subtle planes he spiritualises and distributes. Thus he not only strengthens the personal links which the disciples may have with him but also gives them the privilege of sharing his divine work.[18]

Because of the many spiritual advantages of remembrance, Meher Baba urged his lovers to **entrust your mind to me by remembering me . . . in your heart as often as you can. Remember me so often that your mind is at a loss to find other thoughts to feed on.**[19]

The remedy for all ills is to remember me constantly and wholeheartedly. . . . You will come to remember me wholeheartedly as you remember yourself less and less.[20]

Your being with Me is immaterial. It is My being with you that matters. So keep Me with you always.[21] **Make me your constant companion. Think of me more than you think of your own self. The more you think of me, the more you will realize my love for you.**[22]

Think of me. . . . Try to think of me if you cannot do so.[23]

Remembrance and the Name of God

> *Words, words—but the Name of God*
> *given to the eager and pure disciple by the*
> *precious Guru*
> *is the key which unlocks the doors of words*
> *shut fast on the printed page. . . .*
> *Without the name of God no man*
> *comes to that knowledge which is the true knowledge;*
> *without Guru no man can learn the Name of God.*[24]

Transmitted by Baba's poet-disciple Francis Brabazon, these words point to the most concrete tool for spiritual remembrance—the name of God. References to the holy and sacred name of God occur throughout spiritual history. In Judaism, in Christianity, and in the Bhagavad-Gita, God's name has had a mystic significance, echoed again through the lips of Muhammad:

> *But keep in remembrance*
> *The name of thy Lord*
> *And devote thyself*
> *To Him whole-heartedly.*[25]

God in His infinite aspect is beyond the thoughts and words of the mind. However, the name of God is a reflection of perfection in the finite, a doorway to the infinite.

The mental or oral repetition of God's name is the highest form of a spiritual practice called "mantra" (spiritually charged words or phrases).

***Mantra* is very beneficial to a neophyte on the spiritual path, particularly so when it is given by the Guru. The first and immediate result accruing from the oft repetition of word or words is the concentration of the mind on the subject to be gained. Secondly, the sound vibrations as a result of continuous repetition induce in the course of time an harmonious sympathy to the sound vibrations of the higher planes, engendering a blissful feeling—a factor greatly encouraging to a beginner.**[26]

Baba points out that a mantra has immense possibilities for good as well as bad, depending on the perfection of the guru and mantra. The safest mantra is **the continual repetition of any one name of God, or the continuous thinking and remembrance of God.**[27] To some who inquired about the techniques for mental repetition of God's name, Baba gave an example:

Concentrate your mind on the repetition alone and breathe regularly while doing so. Inhale and exhale the breath slowly and repeat the name of God as you breathe. Let other thoughts come—they will come—but always strive to drive them away; . . . keep the mind cool and steady. Once you have gained a liking for this exercise, you will never drop it but find a secret pleasure in the duty.[28] Elsewhere, Baba hinted that oral repetition is more powerful and thus preferable if privacy is available.

Remembering Meher Baba's Name

In one respect, any name of God is equivalent to any other, whether God the Infinite or God as the God-Man. Of course, the disciple of Meher Baba is encouraged to use Meher Baba's name. "Taking" (or repeating, remembering, thinking of) Meher Baba's name is perhaps the simplest way to practice remembrance and avoid negativity: **Let Baba's name serve as a net around you so that your thoughts, like mosquitoes, may keep buzzing around you and yet not sting you.**[29]

If taking Baba's name is useful in ordinary life, it is especially practical in emergency situations. Two incidents that illustrate the power of the Avatar's name also provoked interesting reactions from Baba. The first story concerns a fifty-five-year-old mother named Jagranidevi. She lived in northern India and was a devoted Baba lover. While collecting grass for her cattle one morning in May 1960, she was viciously attacked by a robber and immediately began crying out to Baba. Soon after, three cows appeared from nowhere and one began attacking the robber, the other two standing on either side of Jagranidevi as if to protect her. The battle continued until a bullock cart came along and the thief fled. Baba was told of her experience and commented, **God is omnipresent, and the one who calls out sincerely to Him never fails to be heard and receive His help.**[30] Another time, a young Baba lover was in a severe motorbike accident but repeated Baba's name as he was flying through the air and miraculously escaped unhurt. The next afternoon he told Baba about what had happened, saying that Baba had saved him. But Baba replied, **Do not attribute the miracle to Me; the miracle was of My Name.**[31]

Ordinarily, the threat of death seems like the greatest emergency. However, Baba cautioned people not to fear leaving the physical body and also revealed the great significance of taking his name at the last moment of life: **I am God, 100% so! There is nothing besides Me. Therefore think only of Me and constantly repeat My Name.**[32] **I say with my Divine Authority to each and all that whosoever takes my name at the time of breathing his last comes to me: so do not forget to remember me in your last moments.**[33]

If you just take my name at the moment of dropping your body, you will come to me. Yes, anyone. It's not easy to take my name at the very moment of leaving the body. Then you individually experience infinite bliss. . . . Even spiritual ecstasy cannot be compared with Divine Bliss. Remember this![34]

As Lord Krishna, Baba made a remarkably similar statement in the Bhagavad-Gita: "And at the time of death, whoever goes forth, abandoning the body, meditating upon Me indeed, he attains to my state; of this no doubt exists. . . . Therefore at all times meditate on Me."[35]

Remembering Meher Baba at the last moment has powerful implications for any Baba lover in the *now*, for, **Unless you start remembering me from now on, it will be difficult to remember me**

when your end approaches. You should start practising from now on. Even if you take my name only once every day, you will not forget to remember me in your dying moments.[36]

Remembering to Remember

> *Wouldn't it be a wonderful thing to have*
> *a friend*
> *who wouldn't want one to beguile time*
> *but would turn on one in kindly anger,*
> *"You bloody loafer—*
> *whatya foolin' about* doing *instead of*
> *being occupied with his Name?"*[37]

Even as the loving guru supplies constant possibilities for remembrance, the gift of effort devolves upon the aspirant:

Just as when we breathe we do not pay attention to our breathing, and in sound sleep it is automatic and our constant companion, and still we do not pay attention to it, so Baba is there *all the time* and therefore you don't feel Him.[38] **Although I am "taking" my own name continuously, I have come to hear it repeated by my lovers, and even though I were deaf, I would hear it if you repeated it only once with all your heart in it. If you cannot remember me constantly, then always take (repeat, think of) my name before going to sleep and on waking up.**[39]

Heartfelt remembrance of Meher Baba's name is not really different from loving him: it is both a cause and a result of the love relationship. The lover automatically remembers the beloved. Conversely, remembering the symbol of perfect love brings that love to oneself. Thus, the technique of remembering the Avatar by taking Meher Baba's name is both a partner to the Master-disciple love relationship and the last resort of an aspirant trying to evoke Baba's method.

If a sincere seeker cannot live a life of wisdom, love, and selfless service, perhaps he can learn about the Avatar. If he cannot surrender to the Avatar, perhaps he can obey Meher Baba's general wishes. If he cannot obey, perhaps he can love Baba. If he cannot love Baba, perhaps he can remember Baba. If he cannot remember Baba, perhaps he can *try* to remember by repeating Baba's name. If

Meher Baba *is* the Avatar of the Age, then this simple practice might be more effective in waking divine inner consciousness than thousands of years of traditional religious observances.

I am in everybody's heart, but I am sleeping there. It is my old, old habit. In order to awaken Me, you should always call out to Me and say, "Baba, Baba, Baba . . ." continuously. Then I, who am asleep in your heart, will not find any pleasure in remaining asleep. Let alone sleep, I shall not find time even to doze . . . I shall slowly be awakened in your heart by hearing your constant call . . . your taking My Name constantly.

Once I am awake in your heart, you too would awake, and remain awake for all time. Therefore repeat My Name constantly and awake Me in your hearts so that you become awake for all time.[40]

CHAPTER 12

Doorways to the Mastery of Consciousness

Each moment with which man is confronted can either tighten the grip of the false or deliver him to the Truth.
—MEHER BABA, *Life at Its Best*

Love, obedience, surrender, remembrance—all in the midst of ordinary life: these are the oldest tenets of practical mysticism. As expounded by Meher Baba, they are the attitudes and practices that can accelerate the mastery of consciousness.

Is it possible to summarize Baba's approach and still capture the mystical essence of its blend of elements? Had I such wisdom, I would not hestitate to try. Lacking it, I can think of few persons more qualified to condense Meher Baba's method than his mandali, that intimate circle of disciples totally committed to Baba for decades. Several of the mandali living in India patiently responded in 1972 and 1975 to my questions about practical techniques. And they were kind enough to review several of the 1972 transcripts. Although I have taken liberties in editing their statements, their original words and meanings are preserved as carefully as possible.

Advice to Newcomers

When asked how persons just learning about Meher Baba should proceed, several mandali gave similar suggestions.

"They should read more about Baba. People who are approaching

Baba intellectually should read about him. If they have a spontaneous love for Baba, then they can rely on their hearts."[1]

"Go to his centers; read his books. It depends on the ripeness and readiness of the *sanskaras*. Baba's call is an inner call; when the ground is ready, they will easily come toward Baba."[2]

"Tell them to read his books. From the books they can find out something about Baba. In the beginning, reading will help, definitely. Then they come into contact with Baba people and they get to talk to them and know more about him. If they are ready, they will get some experience, not in an unusual or supernatural way, but some internal feeling about Baba. If the time is right for such persons, Baba will work with them."[3]

If a new seeker is urged on by an inner response after becoming familiar with Meher Baba, what can he do next?

"I would say that a person should make available for himself all the ways and means of reading about Baba—talking to persons who have had long contact with Baba, contemplating about Baba, meditating about Baba, talking about Baba, and trying to make Baba his constant companion . . . that of course would create love, evoke love for Baba within oneself. And then the understanding comes, after he has love for Baba. To understand is to get closer to him, nearer to him." [4]

"Just tell that person to think about Baba. I do not mean formal meditation. Think of him more and more. Perhaps, in due course, if he is ready, then he will see something about Baba."[5]

"Take Baba's name all the time. Nothing more. He has read the books, so the only thing left is to take Baba's name during all the times of one's life. . . . the feeling will come; Baba will give the feeling."[6]

"Just do nothing but remember Baba, constantly remember Baba. . . . that would be taking one toward Baba. It is not necessary to go to any other saints or sadhus. . . . Gradually Baba will call the person toward him."[7]

Then there is the individual who might be interested enough to read Baba's books and is attracted intellectually, but who gets no feeling or conviction about Baba's path. What of him?

"My advice to him is that he should completely forget about becoming a Baba lover or follower. He should try to lead his life and imbibe the feelings that he gets from Baba lovers he likes, and try to put them into practice into his own life. He should completely forget about loving Baba or believing in him. If he loves anybody, if Baba is Who he really is, then he'll be loving Baba."[8]

"That's Baba's job; the time has to come. Someone is not convinced through what I say or you say, not through anything Baba has written. If, in spite of themselves, they have recognized Him as the One, it's really a recognition. That part of it is Baba's. He has to touch the heart; then whatever I say or you say has meaning, but before that I could sit and talk to somebody through the night and it wouldn't make a dent."[9]

In Tune with Meher Baba's Method

Once an aspirant is drawn to Baba and has a sincere desire to follow him, how should he pursue the Avataric path?

> In the early days we had no literature; we had no books. His discourses and books came at a much later date. So the present generation is very lucky and fortunate to have these things to read, to try to understand. Then the simplest thing for ones who accept Baba as their God is to remember him and try to obey him and try to love him as God.
>
> I don't think it is good to renounce the world. Baba never asked anyone to leave his responsibilities. Baba always said to be in the world, to do your duty faithfully, honestly, and at the same time remember him and feel everything is being done for Baba. . . . The simplest way to remember him is just to meditate on his name and to try to lead whatever life you lead honestly and sincerely, without shirking your responsibility.[10]

Another of Baba's intimates, Meherjee Karkaria, who was instructed to live in the ordinary world, echoed this theme and added:

> Do your duty. Work. At the same time keep Baba at the back of your mind. And never care for the results. Anything you handle, try your best, honestly, sincerely, putting in hard labor. . . .
>
> I feel that to love Baba is to carry out the message that he has left behind. For all these years he has been giving us discourses and everything. If we just keep up with a small part of it, that is loving him.[11]

The picture is enriched by those who lived with Baba and accompanied him on most of his journeys. Asked what Baba would say to "do," Manija S. Irani answered:

What Baba says or would say for people, that's written in books. And if there is such a thing as a method in loving God, then it is written about enough; Baba has given it in words. . . . When you really come down to it, Baba stresses only love, loving God. . . . The only thing that made him happy was love; but not that kind of love we interpret as love. Suppose you love Baba, and so you just sit and gaze at him adoringly. Well, this would not have pleased Baba. Therefore, Baba says obedience is higher than love, because obedience goes even beyond the joy of loving and the thought of self. . . .

It doesn't matter what you take up doing; you are serving Baba. . . . It doesn't matter if you're selling socks or whatever. You love Baba, and somehow that love reaches out through you, brushes onto another. Whatever you are working at, in your heart of hearts you know that you are with him. You're thinking of Baba, you're saying his name, you're loving him. . . . all the time you think of him, not in a forced way but in the natural sense. . . . But you must remember the *way* Baba would want it done. It's not *what* work you do, it's *how* you do it that makes all the difference. And the difference is because you love Baba. . . .

Meditating is remembering Baba every minute by doing what we know would please him.

You talk to Baba, and believe me, he always answers. That's the one thing that makes Baba's presence most felt. We talk to him just like we used to talk to him. He was silent then, and yet he answered; now he's more silent, but he answers more lively and unfailingly each time.[12]

Emerging from these statements is the spiritual paradox of simultaneous effort and resignation. Adi K. Irani expanded that theme:

Completely entrust yourself, read his books, discuss what he has said, argue about it, try to understand, contemplate, meditate. But remember one thing, these things will not give you spiritual position.

It is only your love, it is only your adherence, it is only your understanding, your conviction about him, and your service to him, that will give you a push forward.

All I have to do is submit myself and be the humblest man in the world and say, "Baba, the strings of my life are entirely in your hands, you guide me. Whatever you want me to do I shall do, for the rest of the things, you are responsible."[13]

Your love can be evoked for him provided you learn to give yourself an opportunity to live in the proper conditions. . . . Create the circumstances and the love comes, slowly and gradually.[14]

The technique of integrating remembrance of God with ordinary duties was illustrated by Bhau Kulchuri:

> Baba has given you that meditation which can be put into action. For example, suppose you have a house. You know that this house does not belong to you; it belongs to the Lord. Why do you take care of it and clean it? Because it is given to you. It is the property of the Lord. And of course, the Lord is there.
>
> So this is the practical thing he has given to us. Every action, every thing; just think that it is for the Lord. It becomes so natural.[15]

Implementing Meher Baba's Method

At a certain point on the Avataric path, the seeker's tentative explorations turn into sureness: "Conviction is something very solid. It is a balance between mind and heart. Whatever the heart feels, the mind backs up and whatever the mind thinks, the heart backs up. . . . And that's why I say that this conviction is nothing but God-realization in disguise."[16]

The continuing task for the Baba lover can be expressed ever so directly, as through disciple Sarosh Irani: "I will give you my own opinion. Baba's method is very simple—love, obey, and surrender. That is my whole principle. I obey him to the best of my ability. I give my full surrender to him and accept him as my God."[17]

The mystic path may be simple, but it is not simplistic. Those following the Avatar keep discovering deeper and deeper subtleties in overcoming the veil that separates them from experiencing their unity with God. In discussing the task for aspiring Baba lovers, Eruch Jessawala began to explain such subtleties:

"What Baba wanted was an unadulterated love or remembrance of him. To remember him is to love him, surely. It comes down to that. It brings us so close to him that there comes a point when your remembrances change into glorifying him. Then when you sit down or you're just conversing, you are glorifying him. And that glorification is raised to such a pitch that words fail you. There you are, just lost in glorifying him; you are lost and you find him."[18]

At a certain stage, when the consciousness of God's presence saturates one's entire life, even "remembrance" takes on a subtle aspect. Adi Irani told of a man coming into his office and saying,

"Adi, every time I come in I see you doing work in your office. You are supposed to be remembering Baba, but I don't see you remembering Baba."

Adi replied, "You are perfectly right. Let me explain. I feel the work that I am doing is Baba's. When I sleep he makes me sleep; when I arise it is he who makes me arise. Baba is there in my work, in anything that I do. He is there all the time. I feel Baba in my heart all the time. Do you want me to extract Meher Baba from my heart and throw him at a distance and then start remembering him from there?"[19]

As Eruch Jessawala observed, "Our concept of remembering Baba is so topsy-turvy. Remembering him like 'Baba, Baba, Baba,' or meditating on him, or concentrating on him—that's only the first stage. What helps you remember him continually and constantly is remembering yourself less. Ways and means to remember yourself less are equivalent to remembering him more. That's the real definition. . . . It is he who has lost himself in you. So the more you lose yourself in yourself, the more he shines in you. You see that?"[20]

In a sense, the natural ability to heed Meher Baba's invitation to **Keep me as your constant companion** is both a goal for the aspiring Baba lover and the ultimate technique for the advanced disciple. Orienting one's entire life around God reduces the force of the ego, enabling one better to remember Him and to uncover that divine spark of love which motivates the soul to greater heights of consciousness.

But no matter how clearly the aspirant sees the goal, it always helps to be reminded of practical ways to outfox the ego. On a sun-filled morning atop the hill that overlooks Meherabad, Eruch Jessawala mused about three spiritual "secrets" for the serious seeker.

> The first lesson one has to learn is not to hurt the feelings of anyone else. I recite this of Baba: **"It's my abode—if you hurt the heart, you hurt me there, because I am there."** First try to do that, Baba says, and the secret behind *that* secret is to efface yourself.
>
> There are people in the world who want to find God . . . but He can never be found. It is foolish to try to find Him. Find One who is all-pervading? Who is everywhere? Who is everything? How could you find that which is never lost? So what is needed is not to find Him, but to lose yourself.
>
> How will you lose yourself? There's no way to lose yourself. You start

with *trying* to efface yourself; that means every little thing should be an act of humility, of love. If you remain natural, Baba says that will help you. Then, if one is really natural, automatically, one remains honest, one remains humble, one remains loving.

How can you really efface yourself? Only with the grace of the Perfect Master. And how to win the grace of the Perfect Master is to please him. . . . You can't buy him, you can't serve him, you can't do anything like that. All that is needed is that he should be pleased. And Baba has given us a formula for how we can please him.

So the third secret is to please him. Baba says that there are three things that will please him: **"Think of things that you will not hesitate to think in my presence; speak words that you will not hesitate to speak in my presence, and do things that you will not hesitate to do in my presence."** In short, what he means is to keep his constant company, to feel that he is ever present—which is the fact, which is the reality.

If you can all the time keep his presence, and think, speak, and act as if you are in his presence, you are sure to be on the right path. You are sure to please him.[21]

Perhaps, through these informal conversations, Meher Baba's close disciples have offered a summary of his method. They make clear that to follow the Avatar is to make certain efforts, to adopt certain perspectives, to nurture certain commitments. But the way of the Avatar lies equally in the Beloved's response to the lover.

Asked about further advice after describing ways to get closer to Baba, Arnavaz Dadachanji replied, "Yes, if you do this, there will be an unfoldment within you and Baba will do the rest, and you will know your way. It's in his hands, not in your hands."[22]

Several of Baba's mandali reiterated this extremely important principle: God cannot be coerced. On the path of Meher Baba, the Avatar makes the final decisions. Although it seems that the aspirant makes choices (and he must try to do so), only Baba draws him at precisely the right time for his spiritual development, neither a second early nor a second late. In reality only God can help the aspirant to find himself. In reality the seeker is not different from God.

The humour of the divine love-game is that the One who is sought is Himself the seeker. It is the Sought who prompts the seeker to ask, Where can I find Him whom I seek? The seeker asking, Where is God? is really God saying, Where indeed is the seeker![23]

One of the most difficult realizations on the Avataric path is that all the focus on the Master, all his assistance in awakening consciousness, comes from an unquenchable source of love closer than one's own breath. Meher Baba's method is nothing other than a way to experience such a discovery:

The more you love me, the sooner you will discard the falsehood you have chosen to hide under that hoodwinks you into believing you are what you are not. I am in all and love all equally. Your love for me will wear through your falseness and make you realize the self that you truly are.[24]

PART IV

Reflections on the Way

Introduction

Dear Reader,

Although I hope that Part III gives a usable account of Meher Baba's path, several important and controversial issues deserve further discussion.

Perhaps the most critical issue is Meher Baba's claim of Avatarhood, taken up in Chapter 13. Sooner or later, the Baba lover's assessment of Baba's divinity is crucial. Even for the intellectually curious, Baba's assertions of Godhood may evoke special interest.

Particular concerns have been raised because of Meher Baba's physical passing in 1969. In Chapter 14, I reexamine the viability of following Baba now that he is out of the body. With some trepidation, I analyze other unresolved mysteries that surround Meher Baba's statements and predictions.

Chapter 15 was equally difficult to write and makes me extremely uneasy. In it, I offer a few excerpts and considerable editorial interpretation on the Meher Baba "movement." By its nature, my commentary is speculative, but the curiosity of those attracted to Baba generates predictable questions. With full realization of my lack of special wisdom or spiritual authority, Chapter 15 responds to basic inquiries about the characteristics and possible future of the Meher Baba movement.

CHAPTER 13

Reactions to Meher Baba

Whatever anyone takes me to be, I am that.
—MEHER BABA, *The Awakener*

The spiritual efficacy of Meher Baba's method is entirely dependent on his being the Avatar. To the comparative philosopher Baba's claim to be God might be interesting, but it would not change Baba's metaphysical ideas. However, to the aspirant pursuing Baba's path, the issue becomes supremely important.

If Meher Baba is *really* the Avatar, it cannot be proven by words or testimonials or even miracles. The ultimate confirmation of Baba's divinity requires the inquirer to be God-realized. Even a personal acceptance of Baba as God can come only from deepest intuition, from the inner core of consciousness. As Baba said, **To ask for a purely intellectual proof of the existence of God is like asking for the privilege of being able to see with your ears!**[1]

Baba was straightforward about his identity, anticipated skepticism, and desired honesty in people's reactions. He also reinforced the aspirant's right to test his claims and to measure him against the highest standards fathomable by the human mind. Given the personal nature of evaluating Baba's claim, I offer selected reactions to Baba. These positive personal responses are presented not as evidence, merely as examples of the thousands cataloged in the Baba literature, all consistent with his being the Avatar.

Reflections from the Mind

The mental level of reaction to Meher Baba encompasses reason and the intellect. Despite his mystical approach, Baba is able to generate immense respect from scholars, members of the media, and reasonable people of the Establishment. For example, Dr. W. Y. Evans-Wentz, the great scholar and translator of Asian spiritual works, comments on the "profundity of the author's insight" in Baba's *Life at Its Best,* and writes: "This small, but precious, volume of American-born messages from Meher Baba, the illustrious Sadguru of India, should prove to be, not only to his own disciples, but to all pilgrims who have entered upon the Path, a source of unending inspiration."[2]

In reviewing Baba's most comprehensive book on the metaphysics of consciousness, Dr. Evans-Wentz observed: "Meher Baba's enlightening treatise adds much to the sum total of learning, and contributes incalculably to the enrichment of mankind. . . . No other Teacher in our time or in any known past time has so minutely analyzed consciousness as Meher Baba has in *God Speaks.*"[3]

The news media reacted variously to Baba, including some sensational and cynical newspaper reports. Occasionally, reporters would test Baba only to have their skepticism jolted. On April 10, 1932, reporter James Douglas interviewed Baba in London. He was armed with a questionnaire drawn up by an Oriental scholar, Sir Denison Ross, that was designed to expose Baba as a fraud. After the interview Douglas wrote in the London *Daily Express:* "It [the questionnaire] was designed to trap the teacher, but he smilingly threaded his way through it without stumbling. His mastery of dialectic is consummate. It was quite Socratic in its ease. He frequently put questions to me which startled me by their penetration. But he never evaded a direct question."[4]

But how is a reasonable person to regard Meher Baba's claim to be the returning Avatar? The notion of Avataric reappearance is reasonable according to the messianic expectation of most major religious traditions. As author Irene Conybeare points out:

Even in the Apocryphal New Testament is one passage that says that Zoroaster prophesied the coming of Christ. Moses foretold the advent of Jesus; Mohammed and Jesus alike indicated that they, or one like them, would come again. The followers of Mohammed are now expecting the return of the *Mahdi,* and the Hindus are watching for the Tenth, or *Kalki* Avatar, while Christians look for the Second Advent. Today the Buddhists are gathering together in expectation of the return of the Buddha; for did not Gautama say: "There have been Buddhas after Me. . . ." He also stated: "Two thousand and five hundred years after Me, my law will have known its End. Another Buddha, the greatest of them all, will come into the world. He will regenerate it and establish the New Law."[5]

The cosmic implications of Meher Baba's being the Avatar of this age might seem utterly unreasonable; but,

On the other hand, when one looks at his capacity for organisation, for attention to details, for large-scale direction and movement, for strict punctuality, promptness and quickness of action, for discipline combined with affection and compassion, for attention to the small details of the creature comforts of his lovers whom he invites for meeting him, at public gatherings, on travels, etc.—all these qualities are unquestionably characteristics of a balanced and rational mind—Meher Baba has no equal.[6]

Further reasoned analysis is given by a very successful business executive who described his initial meeting with Baba:

That one week-end with its several opportunities to see him in action was sufficient to convince me that he was hands-down the best story teller with gentle humor (even via the handicap of an alphabet board) I had ever encountered, the best business mind I had known in a life spent working in big business, the best philosopher I had met, and the most sensitively human and loving individual I had ever enjoyed.

Had I decided that he was really the Avatar? I'm sure I would have no means of judging the qualifications and achievements of Avatarhood and further I had found Meher Baba surpassing all of my previous standards of excellence in areas in which I felt competent to judge. . . . But this I can say, my own intuition tells me that I shall never again meet an individual with those profound capabilities and that uncanny ability to satisfy me internally which I found in Meher Baba.[7]

One cannot help but think in retrospect of the millions who knew of Mohammed, and Jesus, and Buddha, but who failed to listen to them because the chance seemed so slight that the Avatar, or even a great spiritual teacher, was really at hand.[8]

Reflections from the Heart

Although Meher Baba encouraged sincere tests of the mind, by far the most powerful impact on his lovers takes place at a feeling level. Whether or not a physical meeting is involved, whether the individual is a poor Asian peasant or a sophisticated Western intellectual, it is the heart that draws most of Baba's lovers. Among the thousands of reports of internal transformations resulting from Baba's contact, the most common theme is his love. Many who had physical or mental contact with Baba reported special moments of exquisite peace, during which they experienced an encompassing abundance of unconditional love. Typical are two reactions, of a man and a woman, each meeting Baba for the first time:

"He smiled, and motioned me to sit beside him. He took my hand and from time to time patted my shoulder. We sat for several minutes in silence and I was aware of a great feeling of love and peace emanating from him; also a curious feeling of recognition came to me, as if I had found a long lost friend."[9]

"My most outstanding impression of that first meeting is one of peering into bottomless pools of infinite love and tenderness, as my eyes met his. . . . I felt that in an inexplicable way he was the reason for my very existence; that I had never really lived until this moment; that he was deeply familiar and precious to me, even as I was no stranger and very dear to him."[10]

Another example, interesting because the individual never met Baba physically, involved a major orchestra's first violinist. He seemed to have lost some vital spark in his performance and was walking down a beach on the verge of suicide because of his increasing failure. Coincidentally, a new Baba lover on the same beach felt impelled to speak to him and left him a little book of Baba's. Later that evening, the violinist opened the book and saw a photograph of Baba. A flash of inner light seemed to penetrate his being and he felt healed of suicidal intent. Resuming practice with the orchestra, he felt the power of the Master sustaining him for the solo part he was scheduled to play. He reported that when he arose to play his solo at the concert, he could see nothing but Baba's luminous face before his eyes, and his whole being was illuminated by Baba's consciousness. A wellspring of emotion and power such as he had never experienced poured out through his fingers in such tonal richness and depth of feeling that the audience rose in a tremendous, spontaneous ovation. After the concert the conductor looked at him in amazement as he heartily commended him for his superlative performance.[11]

Although emotional enthusiasm does not provide hard evidence for the existence of a God-Man, and Baba himself de-emphasized the necessity of spectacular inner experiences, he did have an uncanny ability to touch the very core of being in those he affected:

> Of course, I knew that Baba, as everyone affectionately calls him, had been saying for many years that he was God-Realized, was, in fact, an incarnation of the Godhead, a God-man . . . and I knew that the Sufis and thousands of people everywhere had recognized this claim, but as with Thomas, I had to see for myself.
>
> Well, I had seen; and the cry of the deepest parts of my consciousness had been answered. I was satisfied that if ever it was possible to "see" God on this earth, I had seen Him. And as time went on, the proof that this had not been merely some emotional conversion was shown by the simple fact that a true creativity began in me a few days after this meeting and has continued ever since.[12]

> Whether Meher Baba is the totality of Godhead or not, I have personally no way of knowing—I can only measure to my own degree. But to that degree, he is the embodiment of that ideal which I call God. Since beauty and knowledge has been the only God I have ever worshipped or pursued, and since this man appeals to my eyes as the very embodiment and manifestation of beauty and knowledge, I call him God. Not only the all-forgivingness and humour in his eyes, but the very movements of his hands and body, have unlocked regions within me which were unknown to me before. No man or woman, no flight of thought, no aesthetic experience, no sublimity of nature, has touched the depths of me as this man has. I have met no one, or experienced no experience, which has melted my heart or sharpened my intellect as he has.[13]

The writer, Francis Brabazon, was to become one of Baba's intimate disciples.

Reflections from the Heights

Inspirational experiences do not demonstrate Baba's divinity; they are merely consistent with it. As many mystics point out, one can *know* another's spiritual status only to the extent that he is at an equivalent level. So it is especially interesting to examine the reactions to Baba from those who attained their own spiritual recognition. Around 1929, a confrontation occurred in Iran with a respected head of the Baha'i faith who had come to challenge Baba; "but the moment he saw Baba and felt his touch he forgot his challenge and questions. He wept, and falling prostrate at Baba's feet cried, 'you are God!' Then he rushed out to proclaim to others, 'I have seen God!' All who heard him were much astonished."[14]

Mohandas (Mahatma) Gandhi, one of the great political and inspirational leaders of the twentieth century, came into contact with Baba somewhat unintentionally:

> On 1 September [1931], Baba sailed from Karachi on the *Rajputana* with three of his disciples for England. On the *Rajputana* there was also Mahatma Gandhi on his way to the Indian Round Table Conference. Jamshed Mehta had wired to Gandhi that he should meet Baba. So Gandhi came to Baba's cabin with his secretary, Mahadeo Desai. . . . Gandhi said he had come to see Baba because of the telegram; he would not have come of his own accord, and would stay for five minutes. The meeting lasted for three hours. The next day Gandhi came again. He said, "Baba, it is now time for you to speak and to let the world hear. I feel within me that you are something great." . . . He came a third time and said he would like to spend one night in Baba's cabin.[15]

There were and are advanced souls in the East, much less renowned than Gandhi, but equally significant in the world of true spirituality. Many cases were recorded of beloved saints and yogis of different religious backgrounds recognizing Baba's greatness. Perhaps the most fascinating responses came from the *masts,* those God-intoxicated persons, relatively detached from the physical world as we know it, who experience the higher planes of consciousness.

The late Dr. William Donkin, one of Baba's mandali, wrote an entire volume—*The Wayfarers*—on Baba's extensive work with these spiritually advanced souls, including a rigorously documented chapter on their reactions to Baba. Although Baba traveled incognito, there was an electric recognition of his stature, and numerous *masts* acknowledged his spiritual status.

> CHOTU MIAN (A good mâst of Sangamner) June, 1943. He was brought to Meherabad by Baidul [one of the mandali]. When Baidul met him in

Sangamner, Chotu Mian said to him, "Your prophet is very great; he is greater than Christ and Mahomet, and all the world will believe in him."

SUBHAN MATTU (A good mast of Srinagar, Kashmir) August, 1944. He was brought to the house, and when he saw Baba, he rolled on the ground, and cried out, "He is God."

PIR FAZL SHAH (An adept pilgrim of Kotah) October, 1946. He told Baba, "No one, until you came, has touched my heart with the arrow of Divine Love. You have the power to destroy and flood the whole world. No one fully knows the limits of your greatness; you are the spiritual authority of the time, and if I were to die I would take another body to be close to you."

AZIM KHAN BABA (A high mast of Muttra) October, 1946. When Baba contacted him, he (Azim Khan Baba) said, "You are Allah; you have brought forth the creation, and once in [a] thousand years you come down to see the play of what you have created."

BHORWALA BABA (An adept pilgrim of Bhor) January, 1947. He said of Baba, "Meher Baba has in him the whole universe, he is the Master of everyone, and he is within every disciple. He is this world, that which is above it, and below it; he is in me and in everyone. He is the saint of saints . . . in one glance he sees the whole continent of India."

A MAST [Unnamed] (of the fifth plane, of the "Place of Seclusion") (? May) 1946. He was brought to Baba's house, and when he reached the gate, he said, "We have come to the garden of Paradise (*Gulistan*)." Baba came out of the house, and he gazed at Baba's face, laughed with tears of joy in his eyes, and embraced Baba. Pointing to Baba, he then said to those standing by, "Look at this man's face and forehead. They shine as if the sun were there; can't you recognize who he is?"[16]

In Chapters 1 and 8, reference was made to the reactions of those considered to be Perfect Ones, for example, Sai Baba of Shirdi, Upasni Maharaj of Sakori, and Hazrat Babajan of Poona. One woman told of her first visit to Babajan. Babajan asked her where she had come from. At the reply "From Meher Baba," Babajan exclaimed, "From my beloved Meher! My Son! Some day the whole world will call out 'Meher, Meher!' all the trees will cry out 'Meher,' all the birds will sing 'Meher'!"[17]

Hazrat Babajan's prophecy may not have come to completion before Baba left his physical body, but (uncomfortable as I am in emphasizing the miraculous around Baba) it did seem that nature arranged a temporary response to Baba's Avatarhood. Mecca and its

Kaaba ("The Ancient House") represents the holiest place of pilgrimage for Muslims all over the world. From January 22 to January 28, 1969, unique torrential rains hit the ordinarily arid Saudi Arabian coastline. Flood waters began to build up and finally engulfed the Grand Mosque so that its most holy Kaaba was surrounded by six-foot-high waters. No pilgrim could approach it. Never before in history had the Kaaba been unapproachable. This condition persisted from January 31 to February 7, 1969.[18] Meher Baba left his body on January 31, and his body lay in his tomb for pilgrims to see until February 7, when it was buried. Baba had said that his last Avataric incarnation was as Muhammad. It was as if nature had intervened to point to the new most holy place of pilgrimage, even as Muslim spiritual leaders were puzzling over the meaning of this extraordinary event.

All in all, Meher Baba accepted reactions to his possible divinity as valid in their own way: **He who knows everything displaces nothing. To each one I appear to be what he thinks I am.**[19] Baba knew how unlikely it is for humanity to accept God when he manifests as the Avatar.

It is difficult for the Western mind to accept the concept of God in human form. . . . Though none of you understand me externally in my physical form, I am *within* you—within everybody. . . . I am God undoubtedly. . . . If you cannot accept me as God, that should not worry you. Accept me as a true friend.[20]

CHAPTER 14

Final Declarations

When I drop my body, I shall remain in all who love me. I can never die.

—MEHER BABA, quoted in Purdom, *The God-Man*

Perhaps Meher Baba's claims of divinity can be authenticated only by the intuition of a responsive heart. Even so, his physical passing raised further questions. Did God die? What about Baba's promise to break his Silence? Can Baba still be considered a viable Master? Such questions help crystallize the nature of Baba's method after 1969. With the understanding that thousands of pages could be written, let me offer some key excerpts and some cautious interpretation.

Death and Transition

Undoubtedly, Merwan S. Irani's death on January 31, 1969, came as a shock to followers of Meher Baba, even though his body had been seriously ill. But to Meher Baba, it was no surprise. As cataloged in the *Family Letters* from India in 1968 and summarized by Dr. H. P. Bharucha,[1] Baba had offered many veiled predictions of the coming transition. As Baba's sister related, "Looking back, we find that beloved Baba *had* prepared us, had given us many hints that now stand out glaringly in the light of the Event."[2]

Meher Baba: Still a Functioning Master?

Although consistent with omniscience, Baba's apparent knowledge of the time and manner of his physical passing could be expected even if he were only a moderately advanced soul. More important to the spiritual seeker is Baba's capability to function as a personal Master after leaving the body.

Assuming that Meher Baba *is* the Avatar of this age, his method remains essentially unaffected, for the Avatar *can* take a personal interest in guiding potential disciples in the body or out. From Meher Baba's explanations, God as the Avatar has temporarily relieved Himself from the intense suffering and sacrifice of physical embodiment. But his role as Master of Masters is not interrupted, just as infinity cannot be contained.

I am never born. I never die.[3] Although I am present everywhere eternally in my formless Infinite state, from time to time I take form. This taking of the form and leaving it is termed my physical birth and death. In this sense I am born and [in this sense] **I die when my universal work is finished.[4] Yet I never die. I am always the Ancient One. You should all remember that God alone is real, all else is illusion.[5]**

People generally remain indifferent when I am present among them. They understand and appreciate me more after I drop my body. That is the way whenever I come.[6]

When I discussed this issue with Baba's Indian mandali in 1972, they re-echoed Baba's continuing role. Adi K. Irani said, "As much as God is available to the entire humanity at any time of day or night, it goes without saying that the Avatar is available. . . . The only difference it makes is that he doesn't give us the pleasure of looking at his physical body. Everything else remains the same.[7] The Avatar is never dead. He lives a perpetual God's life in creation and beyond and is the only eternal link between God and man."[8]

A simile was given by Eruch Jessawala: "It is like the sun which never rises and descends. It is when we look at the sun from the rotating earth that we get this impression. In the same way, in cycles of time, the consciousness sees the Avatar occasionally. Consciousness occasionally sees the descent of the Avatar, but the Avatar is always there in reality."[9]

Asked to comment along the same line, Manija Irani reinforced the immanence of Baba as Master:

> God takes on a human form so as to make it easy for us, tangible for us, so that we can express our love for him in a tangible way. . . . Baba's dropping the body does not make it any different.
>
> For instance, Baba has said about himself that even after he drops his body, for a hundred years and even more, his presence is so strong that those who love him and all [others] benefit. It's only a matter of not seeing him, but it is as if he is right here. For a hundred years you get that same benefit, that same force, that same love, that same intensity, as it was when he was physically present; then after that it gradually diminishes until the period when his presence and physical coming again is necessitated. That is why Baba kept repeating, "**Hold on, hold to my *daaman*.**"[10]

As Meher Baba explained, between physical incarnations the Avatar delegates most operational responsibilities to the five functioning Perfect Masters. Thus, Baba relieved himself from the conventional mechanics involved in executing the spiritual affairs of the universe. However, his statements clearly suggest that the Avatar is available to willing aspirants *at any moment in history*. Meher Baba as Avatar maintains full awareness of any disciple's situation, as well as the ability to provide internal guidance when needed.

Meher Baba's Manifestation Reconsidered

Historically, the physical death of the Avatar, occurring in typically mortal fashion, has strained the faith of shakier disciples. To many followers at the time, the worldly deaths of Krishna, Buddha, Jesus, and Muhammad produced puzzlement and confusion.

Perhaps more extensively than Jesus tried to prepare his disciples for the crucifixion, Baba offered both clear and veiled information about future events. In 1954 he gave a long statement, "The Final Declaration," dramatically outlining **that there will be the destruction of three-fourths of the world, that a strange disease will attack my body, that I shall suffer humiliation, that I shall break my silence and speak one Word, the Word of words, that there will be my glorification, and that finally I shall drop my body when I shall be stabbed in the back. . . .**[11]

After the startling announcement, Baba observed that **my lovers and others have been confused, trying to interpret my words in different ways.**[12] He later explained that **whenever I say a thing, I**

naturally use my own "language," and whatsoever is said by me is truth. But, my "language" is such that none can understand or grasp the underlying meaning of what I say. Clarifying his Final Declaration, Baba specified the two predictions that could be understood, the two that could not, and the three that were said **in my own "language" and simultaneously in yours.**[13]

Indeed, Baba's body was attacked by a "strange disease," incomprehensible to several competent physicians. Likewise, Baba's "humiliation" is literally interpretable.

Conversely, his predictions of being "stabbed in the back" and of the "destruction of three-fourths of the world" probably *cannot* be taken literally, their being in Baba's "language" and not ours.

Baba implied that three other statements, concerning the breaking of his Silence, his glorification, and the dropping of his body, might be understood on some levels but not on others. Interestingly, these are precisely the issues that have generated the most confusion for lovers after Baba's physical death. Of these mysterious aspects, Baba said, **Only the fulfillment of events can unfold to you, in due course, the meaning of what is said in my own "language."**[14]

Meher Baba's Warnings

This book is not about to unravel Avataric mysteries. Whatever the intellectual interpretation of the Final Declaration, Meher Baba gave his predictions practical implications.

Time and time again, Baba cautioned his lovers about future events that would test their faith, when they would have to make special efforts to hold to his *daaman*, when he might appear humiliated.

At the time of Jesus, I uttered many warnings, yet none could grasp in advance the necessity of my crucifixion.[15] **The thing is that during the phase of humiliation the circumstances will so array themselves that you won't be aware that my *daaman* has slipped off your hands. At that time, you may even feel justified in leaving me. But if you feel that this should not happen, there is one remedy. You should grasp well all I say and understandingly act up to it.**[16]

Baba hinted at the kind of circumstances that could make Baba lovers feel justified in deserting him: **Just as I am now quite unable to do so many physical things unaided, in spite of an otherwise**

healthy body, I may, at the time of the impending crisis, *become even mentally helpless, without being mentally deranged in the least* [my italics]. **You may then not be able to continue to hold on to my daaman because circumstances will seemingly justify your letting it go. I am infinitely merciful, and so repeat the same thing again and again so that you may remember my words and try your best to cling to me.[17]**

You must stick as close as you can to me or you may find yourselves falling off. Like raindrops on an open umbrella that is twirled round, those that are furthest away are shaken off; those that are really close are unmoved.[18]

Baba's warnings to stick to him in the phase of humiliation appear closely linked to the later confusion over his "death" and the breaking of his Silence. Considering the totality of Baba's statements about his personal future, two likelihoods arise: (1) he was specifying some critical event or series of events that would cast serious doubt on his credibility, and (2) such events would occur *before* he manifested as God. Perhaps the initiation of these events was Baba's dropping the body without having broken his physical silence (or without his silence's being perceived as broken). The fact of physical death fits Baba's warning that he might "become even mentally helpless, without being mentally deranged in the least."

Most Baba lovers expected him to speak before he left his body, and his sudden passing provoked crises of faith. Some could claim that Baba failed to keep his promise to speak the Word. Others could presume that the era of Baba's Masterhood is over and feel sincerely justified in leaving his path. Needless to say, desertion becomes much more likely when the Master is physically absent. Of course, there may well be other humiliations perpetrated on Baba's name, very possibly by the actions of so-called lovers, all of which could serve to weaken previous devotees' grasps on Baba's *daaman*.

The Breaking of Meher Baba's Silence

Even among his worldwide family, the breaking of Baba's Silence is still a mystery. A few feel that Baba broke his Silence but the Word was heard only by the most spiritually advanced. Others explain that Baba has always been speaking through his Silence. Many think that Baba spoke but that the result of his speaking will be gradual, taking time to manifest in a new humanity. Still others believe that Baba has not yet broken his Silence.

Any scholarly analysis to prove one interpretation or another is presumptuous. However, the most dramatic interpretation deserves serious consideration. A reporter once asked Baba, "We have here many excerpts concerning your Silence. Is there any one statement that is more significant than the others?" Baba replied, **There is one. When I break my Silence, the world will come to know that *I am the One whom they were waiting for.*** [19]

It is consistent with Baba's metaphysics that this gigantic burst of love and energy, his speaking the Word, could be released *after* leaving the body of Merwan Irani. It is well within Avataric capability. The Avatar manifested physically to his disciples after leaving the body of Jesus. Indeed, the body-imposed limits of Christhood do restrain the Avatar from using his divine power until after he becomes "uncaged":

The only incomparable miracle I will perform is when I speak. . . . I am like a LION—but at the moment a caged lion. Those who recognize me feel the strength of my power but only in a small degree. When I speak, I will uncage myself; and then you will know my Divine Strength![20] Thus, the Avatar can either manifest after he leaves his physical body or he can take another body in order to speak the Word physically.*

However, no matter which interpretation is preferred by the aspirant, Meher Baba's method remains essentially the same. Of course, if a disciple doubts Baba's divinity because he feels that Baba failed to break his Silence, he may lose hold of Baba's *daaman*. At the other extreme, if a Baba lover is so attached to hearing the upcoming Word that he ignores his current spiritual priorities, he is courting neglect of Baba's path.

Meher Baba was supremely sensitive to the range of future reactions of his lovers. Every once in a while, he swept away inordinate speculation about the mysteries of his Silence and Manifestation and reemphasized what was important. **All will know me when I manifest, but those who know and love me now are the really**

*Baba has mentioned that the Avatar regularly appears in a minor or veiled incarnation when a particular role needs to be filled between major Avataric incarnations. More material explaining such minor incarnations is to be found in *How a Master Works* by Ivy O. Duce (Walnut Creek, Calif., 1975).

fortunate.[21] The world will come to me, for they shall then know who I am. But there is no charm in coming to me after I break my Silence. Blessed are they who come to me now.[22]

I want you to know that I will definitely break my silence; and I want you to cling to my *daaman* till the very end, irrespective of whether I speak or not. I am the Highest of the High, and want you to love me not for any spiritual or material gain, nor for the impending breaking of my silence and my manifestation, but I want you to love me for myself, as being God in human form.[23]

Following Meher Baba Now

Other lingering issues for the aspiring Baba lover have surfaced since Baba dropped his body. These practical problems deal with questions of appropriate behavior for those on the Avataric path.

Meher Baba and Other Spiritual Teachers

Meher Baba's messages are highly congruent with the great mystic teachings of the past and the essential teachings of advanced living spiritual teachers from many traditions. However, according to Baba, the Avataric path is best trod with single-minded concentration. If an aspirant is committed to following Meher Baba, he respects *all* sincere lovers of God as brothers and sisters, whether they be masters or disciples; yet he seeks to follow *only* the spiritual guidance of Meher Baba.

The possible blind alleys of chasing after imperfect teachers have already been discussed. In 1968 Baba ordered Adi K. Irani to write a circular to all Baba lovers warning about phony gurus:

"A true Baba lover must remember the repeated warnings given to all Baba lovers again and again to stay away from persons who feel and assert that they are masters and saints and possess powers to help human beings. . . . Beware of them who exploit spirituality to gain their selfish ends and dupe others in the name of Sadgurus and the Avatar."[24]

Baba's instructions to stay away from those teachers who are authentically advanced may seem more puzzling, especially since Baba assigned a low priority to proselytizing and told lovers not to interfere with their friends' devotion to other saints and masters. However, as related by one of Baba's women mandali, "We cannot benefit by following more than one Master, *even* Perfect Masters. . . . Naturally, we respect all others whom we recognize as His own reflection, but we should hold on to only one—and what better one than The One!"[25]

In Baba's words, **It is best that you stick to me alone. You will be benefitted most by unflinching loyalty in your devotion. If you go on running here and there, you get unnecessarily more involved.**[26] **I am the Emperor. If you belong to Me, you will have access to the Infinite Treasure that is Mine. But if, instead, you go after the guards and servants of the palace (the Sa[i]nts and Sadhus) it is sheer folly on your part!**[27]

When I tell you these things and ask you not to visit other saints, perhaps some of you think, "Is Baba feeling jealous of others?" . . . Being the One Reality, the question of rivalry does not arise for me at all. If I am to be jealous at all, I will have to be jealous of My Own Self.[28]

Aspirants following Baba who are tempted to run off and find another guru merely because Baba's physical body has expired are missing the entire point of the Avataric path. Almost surely pointing to the post-1969 period, Baba advised, **There is no need for my lovers to visit other saints.** ***Stick to me even during the phase of humiliation*** [my italics].[29]

As discussed in Chapter 15, some Baba lovers might be connected with spiritual teachers or advanced souls who are also fully dedicated to the Avatar. Such souls would share acceptance of Baba as Avatar and perceive their role as helping the aspirant to love Baba more completely. Given those exceptions, however, aspirants on Baba's path risk considerable delay in their spiritual progress by involving themselves with other teachers and methods.

Spiritual Life-Styles: Personal Tests

Most of those who follow Baba experience internal difficulties. In addition to the particular test of faith for lovers created by Baba's physical passing, Baba implied that each aspirant is tested by Maya, the force of illusion, at his or her point of greatest vulnerability.

Experience suggests that such tests are subtle and tend to involve one's personal life. So far, at least in the Western world, few Baba lovers have received physical threats challenging their allegiance to Baba. More likely examples would be a renewed craving for drugs, spiritual apathy, or a personal attraction to someone who discourages deep commitment to Baba. Inevitably, some aspirants fail their tests, lose confidence in themselves, and lose hold of Baba's *daaman*. (Here it should be emphasized that leaving Baba does not bring on the wrath of God nor hell or even any particular punishment; it merely represents the temporary loss of an extraordinary spiritual opportunity.) Alternatively, every test can result in a reaffirmation of spiritual priorities and a strengthening of commitment.

Spiritual Life-Styles: Standards of Behavior

More likely than not, spiritual tests will have some relationship to personal decisions and behavior in the world. And, more often than not, leaving Baba involves some form of disobedience. Disobedience creates a block between Master and disciple, reducing the latter's receptivity to inner guidance. But, to be practical, many situations present baffling alternatives, and the disciple finds it hard to interpret Baba's wishes. There is no magic formula or rule book for every personal trial, and a Baba lover must take personal responsibility for his choices. "He has just to apply an understanding about Baba through all the available sources—apply his own mind, his own intuition, his own feeling, and his own logic. If his love for Meher Baba is pure, as much as it should be, I don't think he'll go off the track at all."[30]

Spiritual discrimination becomes especially tricky for some Baba lovers because their ability to obey Baba varies with their maturity on the path. What standards of behavior does Baba expect from his lovers? How does one draw the line between inability to obey and disobedience, between forgiving oneself for natural spiritual weaknesses and rationalizing their expression?

For example, the standards of behavior and aspiration given in the *Discourses* are very high. These discourses were given to totally committed disciples; there was no reason for Baba to compromise his suggestions to them. Still, it would be rather miraculous if a brand-new aspirant could live up to such standards. When Baba suggests ways of living and standards of behavior, they are based on a matter of spiritual efficiency and point to the highest possibilities of human life. Baba did consistently caution aspirants about spiritual dangers related to dishonesty, sexual promiscuity, the nonmedical use of drugs, and the search after imperfect gurus. On the whole, however, Baba gave few inflexible "rules" about conduct. Rather, he stressed the *motives* behind actions, while explaining the spiritual effects of unenlightened behavior.

Although certain principles pertain to everyone for all time, Baba gave many instructions that were tailored to particular individuals or particular groups at certain times. For example, in the *Discourses* Baba explains why mental mastery of one's desires is the spiritually superior method of birth control. Yet Baba never converted this unequivocal fact into rigid dogma. Depending on the situation and spiritual capability of the couple, he sometimes advised the use of contraceptives.

As a Master, Meher Baba is both uncompromising and compassionately reasonable. Perhaps his instructions on general behavior can be summarized as follows: (1) Baba communicated the ideal standards and principles of living; (2) he also acknowledged the spiritual imperfections of aspirants and encouraged them to keep trying even though they continually failed; and (3) he asked his lovers to try their best, apply common sense, and remain sincerely responsive to their deepest intuition.

The aspirant has a considerable task. He must avoid excessive guilt over spiritual inadequacies, convert his failures into learning experiences, and strive to do better in the future. He must be prepared to accept the sufferings that come from selfish actions and yet have confidence in the ultimate success of his journey. On the other hand, he must guard against the careless expression of binding desires, especially when disobedience is rationalized. It is a trick of the ego when the seeker condones unspiritual behavior just because it gains social approval or on the ground that one is spiritually imperfect anyway. Another ruse of the ego is to take refuge in Baba's compassion and forgiveness without trying to grow in love and spiritual reliability. Developing adequate conscience and intuition on Baba's path while fighting off the claims of the limited ego is not simple. But then Baba never implied that his method is easy, just that it is worth every second of the time and energy it requires.

If ever the aspiring Baba lover gets wrapped up in intellectual torment over such issues, he can always try to surrender to Baba and go back to the basic priorities of the Avataric path:

"The Avatar has dropped the body. And how fortunate and blessed we are at this event. He has already told humanity what to do. First and foremost, he said, **'Love me.'** And one who obeys him in this respect has nothing left to obey."[31]

But if the task of following the Avatar has become more difficult because of his physical absence, he may have left some compensation. Discussing the phenomenon of current lovers, his close disciple Eruch Jessawala remarked, "They feel His presence without seeing Him, and I can quite believe that, because I too feel that way. Although I miss Him, I feel His presence without seeing Him."[32]

CHAPTER 15

The Meher Baba Movement

I belong to no religion. My religion is love.
Every heart is my temple.

—MEHER BABA, quoted in
Irani, *Family Letters*

Meher Baba's path is clear. His method remains independent of his embodiment and of the inspiration or insanity of later developments. But if his path is clear, what of his trail?

The following discussion of the Meher Baba movement is intended primarily to smooth the way for those who would like to become more deeply involved. However, it may also be of value to those students of the "new religions" interested in the social and organizational aspects of this spiritual orientation.

Who Is a Baba Lover?

It is very difficult to define a Baba lover. There are no formal or external criteria for followers of Meher Baba, no ceremonial initiation, no fee to be paid, nothing to sign, no membership cards to receive. No formal vows are taken to join the Baba family. No rituals, customs, or dress is required of a Baba lover. There are no mandatory readings, meditations, or meetings. There is no required formal preparation, nor are there "tests" for membership. Nothing in a person's past necessarily disqualifies him or her from being regarded as a Baba lover.

As for internal criteria, some might argue that only a handful of *real* Baba lovers love and obey him as he should be loved and obeyed. Others might contend that thousands of sincere, selfless, God-loving individuals who never heard of Meher Baba are more truly Baba lovers than some self-proclaimed followers. Both statements are probably equally valid. But let us focus on those who consciously aspire to some relationship with Meher Baba. Perhaps the most that can be said is that such Baba lovers exist along a continuum based on the quality of their love, obedience, and commitment to Meher Baba as their Master and Guide. Possibly the true mark of a Baba lover is the quality of his life, will, and heart. Even so, these inner qualities do not confer external status, for Baba discouraged his lovers from judging and criticizing each other.

Those who have tried to dedicate their lives to Meher Baba constitute a tremendous variety in race, religious background, nationality, age, educational background, and personality type. Some would be called eccentric; others would be seen as ordinary people. Baba never quashed variation in personal expression; rather, he stressed the increasing consciousness of unity.

Undoubtedly, there are sincere devotees of Baba who would grate on the reader's nerves, and others who provoke justifiable criticism. But all seekers have problems with their ego, Baba lovers being no exception, and Baba specializes in bringing weaknesses to the surface. Recalling his statement that one of his primary tasks is to "improve the vicious," we must also allow for the additional possibility that Baba might draw to him souls considered somewhat unsavory by other teachers. Although a new follower of Baba can generally expect Baba lovers to exhibit spiritual growth, absence of saintliness does not invalidate Baba's method. As a Master, Baba was more concerned about his disciples' working to slay their personal ego than with building their public image.

Baba often explained to his disciples that he guided them through the involution of consciousness "blindfolded," veiled from the experience of higher planes of consciousness. Probably even those closest lovers destined for quick God-realization experience themselves as merely human. Yet they and many other Baba followers are such jewels of Baba's love that their very contact is inspiring. A great number of seekers have been drawn to Baba's path by a certain magnetic quality in his devotees.

Perhaps most agonizing to the Baba family are spiritual pretenders, persons who declare themselves as Baba lovers but who live in blatant disregard of his message, making no attempt to transcend their hypocrisy. Although Baba said he loves all souls equally despite their failing, new aspirants should emulate the gems rather than the hypocrites on their Avataric journey.

Leadership in the Baba Movement

History records a tragic but common thread—the institutionalization of altered truth. The Avataric incarnations of the past have inspired billions, yet it takes unenlightened humanity only a few centuries to form churches and orthodoxies that disguise God's full message. This is no place to review the mistakes committed by world religions in the name of the Lord. However, since it is so soon after the physical manifestation of a possible new dispenser of truth, readers should be forewarned about any possible religions that may be built around Meher Baba.

Is There a Meher Baba Hierarchy?

When a Master dies, it is natural to think about his successor; but the Avatar does not leave a "chargeman," one who takes over spiritual authority for the Master's followers.

"Meher Baba has not left behind any Chargeman because the Avatar takes human form once between 700 and 1400 years. His Work is for the entire things and beings in Creation. . . . A Perfect Master, when he gives up his body, becomes completely disconnected with the Creation; whereas the Avatar, whether in a human body or not, is always linked with the Creation for the good of humanity, and especially for the good of those who love him."[1]

After Baba's passing, the surviving mandali in India affirmed that they had no special authority, that people should ask them neither to resolve personal matters nor to give spiritual pronouncements and orders. Their declaration has not diminished the immense respect and love felt for the dwindling circle of intimate disciples who lived with Baba and served him selflessly. Visitors to India find their observations, remembrances, advice, and extreme humility invaluable and inspiring. However, even among the closest disciples, there is no "head" of the Baba movement except the Avatar himself. Even Mehera Irani—the most special of the mandali, the woman singled out by Baba for extraordinary spiritual training and personal consideration—does not "succeed" Meher Baba, nor does she sanction herself as being considered a successor. There is no pope, nor can one be appointed or elected without mocking the universality of Baba's Avatarhood.

In many passages Baba reaffirmed that he had not come to build a religion or even a church. According to Baba's explicit messages, *there is absolutely no legitimate basis for a traditional religion to be built around Meher Baba.* Nor is there any justification for the creation of an authoritarian leadership hierarchy that would control the lives or spiritual practices of all Baba lovers.

As stressed in the Hopkinsons' biography,

> Baba realised very well that if he put forward any "new religion," it would inevitably go the way of all the rest. The very people who accepted the new teaching would take it over and "interpret" it, so that inevitably it would be brought down by degrees to the level of the interpreters, and forced to conform to the attitudes and interests of mankind in general. With the "teachers" would come "organisers" who would codify and structure the new religion, place it on a sound financial footing and equip it with churches, temples and a hierarchy of priests. . . . [Baba] was as scathing about church organisations as Jesus was about the scribes and Pharisees, or as he himself was later on about the **"hypocritical saints and masters that now flourish everywhere like poisonous mushrooms."** . . .[2]

Divine authority over the lives of the Avatar's lovers is reserved for the Avatar himself, whether or not he is in human form.

Meher Baba Groups

Since Meher Baba has effectively discouraged any Meher Baba religion, it may seem paradoxical to report group activity among Baba lovers. But it is natural for people of deep common interest to join in celebrating their devotion to God and functioning as channels of information about their Master. It is true that Baba encouraged some individuals and groups to do certain work for his cause or to spread his message. He recognized the spiritual lessons that could be learned from cooperative group work, and the organizational necessity for local centers. Yet he reminded Baba groups that organizational work was entirely dispensable, especially if honesty and a loving, cooperative spirit were absent among workers.

When you spread my eternal message of love to others, show them first that you really love me. Do not merely make them read my books and messages. Do more. Live such a life of love, sacrifice, forgiveness, and tolerance that others will love me. If instead of doing the real work of love, you start doing organized propaganda work for me, it is absurd. I need no propaganda or publicity. I do not want propaganda and publicity, but I do want love and honesty. If you cannot live the life of love and honesty, you should stop working for me.[3]

Involvement in service for Baba does carry spiritual advantages *if* it fosters selflessness and additional focus on Baba. But Baba occasionally reminded his workers that, as God, he needed no one to get his work done. **He who works for me, does not oblige me, for he works for his own self.**[4] **My greatness cannot be established in the crowds and through the crowds, but even a few with love can make the masses feel my greatness, and keep the greatness established in their hearts. One single person who really loves me can move the whole world.**[5]

The mid and late 1960s saw an intensification of group efforts in the Western world, partly because of increasing interest in Baba and partly because Baba began encouraging lovers to spread his message of love and truth. Near the end of his physical manifestation, Baba hinted that it was important for more people to become aware of him, but he discouraged his lovers from fanaticism or attempts to convert others. Thus the role of Baba groups is not necessarily to gather new followers; according to Baba, he is the only one who can really do that.

Typically, local Baba groups vary in organizational structure, but they all have leadership by majority consensus. They often conduct open meetings featuring such activities as reading Baba's discourses, showing films, listening to recorded talks about Baba, conducting group discussions, singing, and so forth. Some centers publish and distribute literature by and about Baba. (A list of the major informational outlets is given in Appendix D.)

Ultimately, an aspirant's relationship with Baba is a very personal concern, and there are sincere Baba lovers who feel more comfortable with no group involvement whatsoever. No Meher Baba group can validly dictate what is proper for Baba lovers; it can only share its accumulated experience on Baba's path.

Special Observances

There are very few religious observances among Baba lovers, none mandatory. There are no prescibed holidays, although three dates have special significance. One is the birthday of Baba's body, February 25. Occasionally, Baba groups across the world stage public birthday celebrations, ranging from mass feedings of the poor to musical and dramatic productions.

Another important day is July 10 (often called "Silence Day"), the date in 1925 when Baba initiated his physical silence. For many years, Baba requested his lovers to keep complete silence (or partial fast) on July 10 if it was practical for them. It is likely that the practice of keeping silence or fasting on July 10 will be continued by many out of love and respect for Baba. Yet, to the best of my knowledge, nowhere did Baba order such a practice to continue after he dropped his body, and it seems likely that he would not want the practice permanently ritualized. January 31 is becoming a third important day of commemoration: it is the date on which Baba dropped his physical body. Since 1969 major pilgrimages have been made to Baba's tomb around this time, recently called the *Amartithi* ("Eternal Date").

At meetings, visitors to Baba groups may hear the "Master's Prayer" and the "Prayer of Repentance" being recited. Meher Baba loved music, and songs of every musical idiom have been dedicated to him. Certain groups have favorites that are sung at Baba meetings. There is no secret language, though a newcomer may be baffled by words that have no English equivalent. The most idiosyncratic expression by Baba lovers in the 1970s is the phrase *Jai Baba* (*Jai* pronounced to rhyme with "may" or "my"). It is a short form of the longer Indian phrase *Avatar Meher Baba Ki Jai*, loosely meaning, "Hail (victory) to Avatar Meher Baba!" The phrase is most often used as a substitute for "good-bye," as an initial greeting, or when its original meaning is called for.

Another predictable development has been the upsurge in personal ornamentation with Baba's name or photograph. Buttons, pins, rings, pendants, may be gentle remembrances of the Master for the sincere wearer. However, ornamentation is ultimately a matter of taste and no indication of one's internal spiritual state.

Meher Baba Centers

There are relatively few geographically stable centers devoted solely to Meher Baba. The obvious ones are Meherabad, the location of Baba's tomb; and nearby Meherazad, Baba's ashram—both near Ahmednagar, Maharashtra State. The Avatar Meher Baba Trust, an Indian charity chartered by Baba and administered primarily by his mandali, manages these properties as well as the material needs of those who were dependent on Baba.

In the early 1940s, Baba asked that a suitable spiritual center be found in America; eventually, five hundred acres of ocean-front property in Myrtle Beach, South Carolina, were developed as the Meher Spiritual Center. Baba spent much of his time in the United States in 1952, 1956, and 1958 at the Center, and many have reported feeling his presence and love there.

The sites in and around Ahmednagar and the Myrtle Beach Center are at present the only major Baba centers with consistent residential facilities for visitors. There are many other active groups in Eastern and Western cities. A few have acreage or a building; some rent meeting facilities; and others meet in private homes. Most of the Baba centers in Asia are in different parts of India. An important center for the Australian continent is Avatar's Abode—acreage and residences in Queensland—a site Baba visited and the current home of poet-disciple Francis Brabazon. In Europe, the Meher Baba centers in London have been the most active and influential. In the United States, there are more or less organized Baba centers in many localities, especially in the major urban areas.

One Meher Baba center needs special discussion because it is the only known organization that has Meher Baba's authorization to offer direct spiritual instruction under a teacher. Among the organized disciplines founded on true mysticism is a long line of spiritual orders now called the Sufis. Although secular historians tend to link Sufism with the appearance of Muhammad, Sufi schools share a common heritage with that of ancient Zoroastrianism, esoteric Vedanta, mystic Buddhism, and mystic Christianity. Typically, the most advanced Sufis in any age have recognized the

Avatar and allied themselves with him, taking on characteristics of his inner teachings.

Meher Baba pointed out that Sufi students cannot be guaranteed spiritual benefit unless the order is supervised by a teacher (murshid or murshida) possessing true sainthood or illumination. The rarity of an illumined murshid has led to the emasculation of Sufi instruction, with such groups becoming merely intellectual sects.

A more extensive account of the link between Meher Baba and the American Sufi order, first established by the great Sufi teacher Hazrat Inayat Khan, is found in the pamphlet *Sufism.*[6] Briefly, Hazrat Inayat Khan was sent from Baroda, India, by his master to establish the Sufi message in the Western world. He accomplished his mission and before dropping his body in 1927 gave over his spiritual "charge" and the order's leadership to Ada ("Rabia") Martin. Inayat Khan's selection of an American Jewish woman shocked many of the Europeans associated with his order and most of them split off from her, leaving Murshida Martin to work with a much smaller group. A few years before she died, Murshida Martin learned of Meher Baba, corresponded with him, and felt that he was the *Qutub-e-Irshad*, the reigning Perfect Master in charge of the spiritual hierarchy. Around that time she appointed Ivy Oneita Duce as the next Murshida of the order.

Murshida Duce arrived in India in January 1948 and was immediately convinced that Baba *was* that *Qutub*. Baba confirmed her title and destiny and told her to take charge of the Sufi work in North and South America. Baba said that as long as she remained honest, he would do her work for her, would protect her students from her making any mistakes with them, and would prevent her from taking on any of the karma of her students. He said, **You have to go home and re-establish this work all over again, and I want it on a safe, sound and stable basis so that it will last 600–700 years.**[7] In 1952, Meher Baba rewrote the Sufi Charter and constitution. **I intend to make one unique Charter regarding this reoriented Sufism and send it to Ivy Duce from India in November, with my signature, and entrust the American Sufism work to her. . . . Now when I send the Charter and the Constitution, and the instructions, it will be applicable to the whole Sufi world—and will, by God's Grace—be lasting in its effect and influence.**[8]

Baba expressed his willingness to reorient other schools of authentic mysticism, suggesting the Sufi charter as a prototype for these other paths. Noting elsewhere that it was not necessary to join an authentic organized path in order to follow the Avatar, he commented: **All these ends (the various spiritual paths) mean becoming one with God and living the life of God, in short, deification. But, as I say, the time is such that these rivers have gone dry and so the Ocean itself has to go out and flood these rivers. So it is now time for me to re-orient these different isms which end in one God. . . . The fact that I am connected with all isms and yet detached and above all isms, lays bare the truth that Sufism Reoriented, emanating from me, to be conceived and practiced, will forge out into one of the few pure channels leading to One God.**[9]

Baba promised to be responsible for Murshida Duce's teaching role without disclosing her spiritual status or plane of consciousness. However, he also strongly implied that future murshids of this order (most recently based in Walnut Creek, California) would enjoy at least sixth-plane consciousness, presumably experiencing their illumination consciously.

Since members of Sufism Reoriented promise faith and trust in the Murshid, obedience being necessary for the inner development of the Sufi student, some Baba lovers are puzzled about an apparent dual allegiance. However, Baba's orders regarding Sufism Reoriented allow it to be a direct agency of the Avatar. Thus, there is no contradiction between the guidance of the Murshid and the guidance of Meher Baba. It is the function of the Murshid to help these Sufis to love Baba more completely and to increase spiritual discrimination in order to express his love in the ordinary world. As charted by Meher Baba, Sufism Reoriented must keep pure his message as well as preserve the eternal Sufi teachings of love for God.

The Future of the Meher Baba Movement

Any attempt to predict the ultimate future of the Baba movement involves massive speculation. The movement's direction will depend on events yet to emerge, such as the timing and scope of Baba's manifestation. However, there are some predictable possibilities for the near future.

On the positive side, if Meher Baba really is the Avatar of this age, God in human form, his name and message should continue to spread. More individuals will find their minds and hearts touched by the truth and love of Baba's life and messages. Much initial activity will be generated from the English-speaking nations. Baba once mentioned that America would spark the resurgence of spirituality in the world.

Then there is the negative aspect. If the number of Baba lovers increases dramatically, systematic resistance and criticism may emanate from traditional religious organizations that feel threatened by a "competing" Messiah—ironically, by their own Messiah returned in different form. However, as Baba said as early as 1932, **My work will arouse great enthusiasm and a certain amount of opposition—that is inevitable. But spiritual work is strengthened by opposition, and so it will be with mine. It is like shooting an arrow from a bow—the more you pull the bow-string towards you, the swifter the arrow speeds to its goal.**[10]

Further, despite Baba's injunctions, a quasi religion or quasi hierarchy might sometime be built around Meher Baba's name. It is to be hoped that lovers who understand Baba's message will resist ritualization, dogmatism, or rigid orthodoxy surrounding Baba's incarnation.

Predictable also is increased friction, schism, and organizational competition among segments of the Baba community. Baba's statements about his humiliation and the frailties of the human ego imply that further disruption is probably inevitable. Baba seemed to stimulate difficult group situations in order to bring spiritual weaknesses and strengths to the surface. However, his physical presence and authority prevented many gross distortions and hypocrisies from getting out of hand. With Baba out of the body, aspirants have more room to err and indulge their egoistic inclinations. If Baba is the Avatar, he is no less aware of such events; seekers merely have more latitude for learning through spiritual stupidity.

We can expect valuable historical additions to the Meher Baba literature, although Baba's direct messages and discourses are so lucid and comprehensive that few aspirants will need to become dependent on speculative extrapolations (including the editorial comments in this book). Future books or articles may be helpful in stimulating a deeper appreciation of Meher Baba's path, or they may confuse and mislead aspirants, but no such interpretive work is "gospel." If there are scriptures in the Baba movement, they are Baba's words—not words about Baba's words.

Ultimately, the future of the Baba movement depends on the validity of Meher Baba's identity as Avatar. If Baba's message spreads and more souls are moved by love for him, it will not be the result of spiritual gimmickry, fanatical conversion phenomena, or comfortingly rigid dogma. In the event that Baba was not communicating the truth, there is every likelihood that the Meher Baba movement will fade into historical oblivion as one small tree in a forest of twentieth-century spiritual events.

But if the Avatar has again taken an incarnation, this time as Meher Baba, it is well to remember that his main work is for all those who suffer pangs of spiritual hunger, not merely those souls who know of him or recognize him as the God-Man. According to Baba, it has been his task to revivify the spiritual spark for *everyone* at *every* level, whatever his or her spiritual allegiance. God cares about the quality of the heart, not the intellectual structure of belief systems.

To all, Meher Baba offers a special path and method for those receptive to Avataric guidance and constantly repeats his call:

Age after age, when the wick of Righteousness burns low, the Avatar comes yet once again to rekindle the torch of Love and Truth. Age after age, amidst the clamor of disruptions, wars, fear and chaos, rings the Avatar's call: "COME ALL UNTO ME."

Although, because of the veil of illusion, this Call of the Ancient One may appear as a voice in the wilderness, its echo and re-echo nevertheless pervades through time and space, to rouse at first a few, and eventually millions, from their deep slumber of ignorance. And in the midst of illusion, as the Voice behind all voices, it awakens humanity to bear witness to the Manifestation of God amidst mankind.

The time is come. I repeat the Call and bid all come unto me.

This time-honoured Call of mine thrills the hearts of those who have patiently endured all in their love for God, loving God only for love of God. There are those who fear and shudder at its reverberations, and would flee or resist. And there are yet others who, baffled, fail to understand why the Highest of the High, who is all-sufficient, need necessarily give this Call to humanity.

Irrespective of doubts and convictions, and for the Infinite Love

I bear for one and all, I continue to come as the Avatar, to be judged time and again by humanity in its ignorance, in order to help man distinguish the Real from the false.

Invariably muffled in the cloak of the infinitely true humility of the Ancient One, the Divine Call is at first little heeded, until, in its infinite strength it spreads in volume to reverberate and keep on reverberating in countless hearts as the Voice of Reality. . . .

I give you all my Blessing that the spark of my divine love may implant in your hearts the deep longing for love of God.[11]

Appendices

Introduction to the End of the Beginning

Dear Reader,

At this point I offer supplementary material intended to help the curious follow up their interest in the path of Meher Baba. Appendix A consists of some prayers that Baba dictated and that were referred to earlier in the book. Appendix B is a glossary of unfamiliar terms found in this book and in other publications related to Baba. Appendix C, an annotated bibliography, briefly describes the most important literature by and about Meher Baba. A list of major sources of information about Meher Baba is given in Appendix D, including the locations of major Baba centers and groups.

I realize many people will be reading this book at a time well after the supplement was written. If the need becomes apparent, I plan to prepare a second edition of this book, and I sincerely invite readers to send to me their criticisms, suggestions for additional material, or general reactions. If anyone has trouble locating Baba books or groups, I will try to help. If there are questions about Baba or his method that seem unanswered here, I would be glad either to attempt a response or to find a wiser Baba lover who might be able to give an appropriate reply. Any communications can be sent to: Dr. Allan Cohen, *Mastery of Consciousness*, Harper & Row, Publishers, 10 East 53rd Street, New York, New York 10022, U.S.A., or Dr. Allan Cohen, 24 Bradnell Avenue, Le Roy, New York 14482, U.S.A.

Godspeed!

APPENDIX A

Prayers

Meher Baba dictated a few prayers for possible use by his lovers. For Baba's method the recitation of these prayers is entirely optional, but they may be useful for aspirants who want to express themselves in a structured way. The two most repeated prayers are the "Prayer of Repentance" (its meaning is self-evident) and the "Master's Prayer," in praise of God the Almighty. (For any prayer "I" may be substituted for "We" whenever appropriate.)

The Prayer of Repentance

We repent, O God most merciful; for all our sins; for every thought that was false or unjust or unclean; for every word spoken that ought not to have been spoken; for every deed done that ought not to have been done.

We repent for every deed and word and thought inspired by selfishness, and for every deed and word and thought inspired by hatred.

We repent most specially for every lustful thought and every lustful action; for every lie; for all hypocrisy; for every promise given but not fulfilled, and for all slander and backbiting.

Most specially also, we repent for every action that has brought ruin to others; for every word and deed that has given others pain; and for every wish that pain should befall others.

In your unbounded mercy, we ask you to forgive us, O God, for all these sins committed by us, and to forgive us for our constant failures to think and speak and act according to your will.

The Master's Prayer

O Parvardigar, the Preserver and Protector of All,
You are without Beginning and without End;
Non-dual, beyond comparison; and none can measure You.
You are without color, without expression, without form, and without attributes.
You are unlimited and unfathomable, beyond imagination and conception; eternal and imperishable.
You are indivisible; and none can see you but with eyes Divine.
You always were, You always are, and You always will be;
You are everywhere, You are in everything; and You are also beyond everywhere and beyond everything.
You are in the firmament and in the depths, You are manifest and unmanifest; on all planes, and beyond all planes.
You are in the three worlds, and also beyond the three worlds. You are imperceptible and independent.
You are the Creator, the Lord of Lords, the Knower of all minds and hearts; You are Omnipotent and Omnipresent.
You are Knowledge Infinite, Power Infinite and Bliss Infinite.
You are the Ocean of Knowledge, All-Knowing, Infinitely Knowing; the Knower of the past, the present, and the future; and You are Knowledge itself.
You are All-merciful and eternally benevolent.
You are the Soul of souls, the One with infinite attributes.
You are the Trinity of Truth, Knowledge, and Bliss;
You are the Source of Truth; the Ocean of Love.
You are the Ancient One, the Highest of the High; You are Prabhu and Parameshwar; You are the Beyond-God, and the Beyond-Beyond-God also; You are Parabrahma; Allah; Elahi; Yezdan; Ahuramazda; and God the Beloved.
You are named Ezad: the Only One worthy of worship.

Readers may enjoy one more small prayer dictated for Baba lovers in 1959:

> ***Beloved God, help us all***
> ***To love You more and more,***
> ***And more and more,***
> ***And still yet more,***
> ***Till we become worthy of union with You;***
> ***And help us all to hold fast***
> ***To Baba's*** **daaman** ***til the very end.***

APPENDIX B

Glossary

This glossary defines unfamiliar terms used in the book. Where possible, definitions were adapted from the glossary of *God Speaks* (2nd edition), which was personally approved by Meher Baba.

arti A devotional song; a song in praise of God.

ashram Abode; spiritual center.

atma, atman The individualized soul that is really identical with Paramatma, the Oversoul.

Avatar The Christ; the Saviour; the Ancient One; the descent of God into human form; adj. Avataric.

Bhagavad-Gita Sacred book of the Hindus, featuring the teachings of the Avatar as Krishna.

bhakti Deep devotion; intense love.

bhakti-yoga The yoga or path of love or devotion.

daaman Literally, the hem of a garment. Symbolically ("holding" or "holding on to" the *daaman*), the process of holding on to the Master.

darshan, darshana Literally, seeing; audience. The audience given by a Master to bestow blessings on devotees, sometimes in the form of *prasad*.

dervish A wandering Sufi, usually one with very few possessions.

dnyana-marga The way of knowledge. (Usually appears, in works other than by or about Baba, as "dhyana-marga.")

dnyan-yoga The yoga or path of knowledge. (Usually appears, in works other than by or about Baba, as "dhyan-yoga.")

elevation Levitation as a result of psychic powers.

ganja Cannabis; marijuana or hashish.

guru A spiritual teacher, guide, or master.

hal A spiritual trance bringing ecstasy.

hatha-yoga Self-mortifying ascetism; yoga postures.

jap, japa Repetition, generally of mantras or prayers.

karma Literally, action. Fate; the natural and necessary happenings in one's lifetime, determined by one's past lives or past actions.

karma-marga The way of action.

karma-yoga The yoga or path of action.

kundalini The vital force or power, residing near the base of the spine.

maharishi An advanced spiritual teacher.

mahatma A great soul.

mahayogi A yogi on a higher plane of consciousness.

manas Literally, mind. Also the mental body.

mandali The members of Meher Baba's circle; Baba's close disciples.

mantra A sacred name or phrase, given by a master to his disciple to be repeated as a spiritual discipline.

mast A God-intoxicated soul on the Path, usually on a higher plane of consciousness.

Maya Literally, illusion; false attachment; that which makes the nothing appear as everything; the root of ignorance; the shadow of God; adj. *Mayavic.*

mukti Liberation; release from the cycle of births and deaths.

Murshid (m.), **Murshida** (f.) The spiritual director of a Sufi order; *lowercase,* Sufi religious teacher, advanced spiritual guide.

nirvana The first stage of the final annihilation of limited mind and self; the experience that precedes Realization.

obsession The intrusion of a disincarnate spirit on the thoughts and actions of a vulnerable person.

Paramatma, Paramatman Almighty God, the Oversoul.

Parvardigar The Preserver or Sustainer.

possession The total displacement of a vulnerable person's consciousness by a discarnate spirit.

prana Literally, vital energy; the subtle body; also Breath of all life.

pranayama A form of yoga featuring breathing exercises and the possible awakening of the kundalini.

prasad A small gift, usually edible, given by the Master as a concrete expression of his love that, when swallowed, acts as a seed that will eventually grow into full-blown love; a gracious gift of the Master.

Qutub Literally, the hub or axis; a Perfect Master.

Qutub-e-Irshad The head of the five living *Qutubs* who directs the affairs of the universe. In an Avataric age this office is filled by the Avatar.

raja-yoga Yoga by means of meditation and contemplation.

Ram, Rama An incarnation of the Avatar; the subject of the Hindu epic the Ramayana.

rishi Literally, seer. An inspired sage or religious poet.

Sadguru A Perfect Master.

sadhaka One who traverses the path; an aspirant.

sadhana Practice; striving; endeavor.

sadhu A pilgrim; an advanced soul.

sahavas A gathering held by the Master so that his devotees may enjoy his company, that is, his physical presence.

samadhi Temporary stilling of the mind; trance induced by spiritual meditation or other practices.

sanskara Impression; also an impression that is left on the soul as a memory from a former life and that determines one's desires and actions in the present lifetime. (Usually appears, in works other than by or about Baba, as "samskara.")

sanyasi One who has renounced the world.

sharira Literally, body. The gross body.

siddhi A divine power; also an occult power.

subtle Pertaining to the body of energy (subtle body), the world of energy (subtle world), or the experience of the world of energy (subtle consciousness).

Vedanta A philosophy and spiritual practice based on the essence of the four Vedas and on sacred books written later, including the Upanishads.

wali Literally, friend; frequently used in a more restricted sense to mean a saint.

yoga Literally, union. A way of traversing the Path toward union.

yoga-marga The way of yoga.

yogi One who traverses the Path.

APPENDIX C

Annotated Bibliography

This list includes publications related to Meher Baba as of mid-1977. Some titles may go out of print. However, publishers specializing in Meher Baba literature—Sufism Reoriented, Meher Baba Information, Sheriar Press—often stock back copies. They also issue updated book lists offering new publications. Where the publisher is not the major distributor, I have included that additional information. The current addresses of the major publishers and distributors follow.

Publishers and Distributors

Harper & Row Publishers, Inc.
(Harper Colophon Books and Perennial Library)
10 East 53rd Street
New York, New York 10022, U.S.A.

Meher Baba Information, Inc.
(John F. Kennedy University Press and Beguine Library)
P.O. Box 1101
Berkeley, California 94701, U.S.A.

Sheriar Press, Inc.
P.O. Drawer 1519
North Myrtle Beach, South Carolina 29582, U.S.A.

Sufism Reoriented, Inc.
1300 Boulevard Way
Walnut Creek, California 94595, U.S.A.

Many major titles are available also at local metaphysical bookstores, Baba centers, or through information centers such as those listed in Appendix C.

Works by Meher Baba

Beams from Meher Baba on the Spiritual Panorama. New York: Harper & Row, Perennial Library, 1971. (Softcover, 116 pp.) Originally published San Francisco: Sufism Reoriented, 1958. (Hardcover, 88 pp.) Baba answers questions on such subjects as prayer, obsession, evil, fraudulent saints, and so forth.

Darshan Hours. Berkeley, Calif.: Meher Baba Information, Beguine Library, 1973. (Hardcover & softcover, 72 pp.) Contains Baba's conversations with various lovers in 1962. Not so much a book of teachings as the Master instructing his close ones in the way of love and surrender to him.

Discourses. 6th ed. 3 vols. San Francisco: Sufism Reoriented, 1967. (Softcover, 546 pp.) Original discourses given to disciples between 1938 and 1944. Perhaps the most comprehensive source of Baba's suggestions about the practical details of the spiritual path, covering an immense range of topics. The 1967 edition was personally reviewed and approved by Meher Baba.

The Everything and the Nothing. Berkeley, Calif.: Meher Baba Information, Beguine Library, 1971. (Softcover, 115 pp.) Originally published in Australia, 1963. Contains some of Baba's most recent short discourses. Rich and poetic; highlights the essence of the spiritual high roads with parable, anecdote, and new images.

God in a Pill? Meher Baba on L.S.D. and the High Roads. San Francisco: Sufism Reoriented, 1966. (Pamphlet, 14 pp.) A small pamphlet featuring comments by Baba on the drug scene, taken from several letters dictated by him on the subject.

God Speaks. 2nd ed., rev. New York: Dodd, Mead & Co., 1973. (Hardcover, 334 pp.) A titanic work on the theme of creation and its purpose. Directly dictated by Meher Baba, it describes creation, evolution, reincarnation, involution, and realization—the fundamental mechanics of life and the universe. The second edition incorporates further clarification given by Baba before he dropped his body, including several charts and a glossary approved by him. Not usually the best introductory book because of its complexity, but extremely powerful in scope and execution.

Life at Its Best. Edited by Ivy O. Duce. New York: Harper & Row, Perennial Library, 1972. (Softcover, 106 pp.) A collection of messages given by Baba during his three-week visit to the United States in 1956. Over fifty succinct and penetrating comments on a variety of spiritual topics.

Listen, Humanity. Narrated and edited by D. E. Stevens. New York: Harper & Row, Harper Colophon Books, 1971. (Softcover, 262 pp.) An American businessman describes an intimate gathering with Meher Baba in India in 1955. Part II contains important discourses on life and death, war, suicide, love, and other topics. The last part includes some of Baba's key statements about Avatarhood and his reminiscences.

The Path of Love. Edited by Filis Frederick. New York: Samuel Weiser, 1976. (Softcover, 102 pp.) Discourses, messages, and talks by Meher Baba on such topics as discipleship, the spiritual path, the God-Man or Avatar, and God-realization. All reprinted from *The Awakener* magazine.

Sparks from Meher Baba. Myrtle Beach, S.C.: Friends of Meher Baba, 1962. (Pamphlet, 24 pp.) Distributed by Sheriar Press. Evocative paragraphs from Baba's statements.

Works about Meher Baba

Abdullah, Abdul Kareem (Ramjoo). *Sobs and Throbs or Some Spiritual Highlights.* Phoenix: Avatar Meher Baba Center, 1969. (Softcover, 88 pp.) A moving personal account, originally published in 1929, of events surrounding the Prem ("Love") Ashram that Baba started in the late 1920s. It chronicles some extraordinary spiritual adventures of the young students. Republished in a forthcoming volume that will include Abdullah's diary, recounting the period before and after the events narrated in *Sobs and Throbs.*

Adriel, Jean. *Avatar.* Berkeley, Calif.: John F. Kennedy University

Press, 1971. (Softcover, 284 pp.) An account of the author's personal experiences with Baba from 1931 to 1947 with intermittent discussion of his life and teachings. A very colorful, behind-the-scenes biography of Baba and his activities.

The Answer: Conversations with Meher Baba. Edited by Naosherwan Anzar. Bombay: Glow Publications, 1972. (Softcover, 64 pp.) Available through Meher Baba bookstores and information centers. Transcribed interviews between Baba and questioners in India and Europe from 1931 to 1939. Most of the conversations are unpublished elsewhere.

Anzar, Naosherwan. *The Beloved: The Life and Work of Meher Baba.* North Myrtle Beach, S.C.: Sheriar Press, 1974. (Hardcover, 146 pp.) A most attractive short anecdotal biography laced with Baba quotes and scores of photographs.

Bharucha, Dr. H. P. *Meher Baba's Last Sahavas.* Navsari, India: Dr. H. P. Bharucha, 1969. (Softcover, 48 pp.) Distributed by some Baba bookstores and information centers. A relatively comprehensive account of the weeks and days before Baba dropped his body, along with a narrative of the days afterward and Baba's statements about such an event.

———. *Meher Baba: The Compassionate Father.* Navsari, India: Dr. H. P. Bharucha, 1972. (Softcover, 107 pp.) Stories of extraordinary happenings to persons associated with Baba. Accounts especially reflect Baba's compassion and love for humanity.

Brabazon, Francis. *The East-West Gathering.* Sydney: Meher House Publications, 1963. (Hardcover, 50 pp.) Distributed by Meher Baba Information. An account, in prose and verse, of a significant gathering with Baba and his lovers from the East and the West in 1962.

———. *Journey with God and Messages of Meher Baba.* North Myrtle Beach, S.C.: Sheriar Press, 1971. (Softcover, 35 pp.) A poetic account of the author's visit to India in 1954 to be with Baba; also includes selected messages from Meher Baba.

———. *Stay With God.* Sydney: Garuda Books, 1959. (Hardcover, 167 pp.) An epic narrative in prose and poetry written at Baba's direction. In language of great beauty, Brabazon portrays the advent of the Avatar in our time and his mission of liberation. Of it Baba said, **The book contains food for the brain and a feast for the heart.**

Conybeare, Irene. *In Quest of Truth, or How I Came to Meher Baba.* Kakinada, India: S.S.P. Udaseen, circa 1960. (Softcover, 311 pp.) An autobiographical account of a Baba lover with comments on facets of spirituality.

Deshmukh, Dr. Chakradar. *Sparks of the Truth from Dissertations of Meher Baba.* North Myrtle Beach, S.C.: Sheriar Press, 1971. (Softcover, 96 pp.) Dr. Deshmukh's versions of discourses heard in Baba's presence. They were not reviewed by Baba but reflect much of his imagery and intent.

Donkin, William. *The Wayfarers.* San Francisco: Sufism Reoriented, 1969. (Hardcover, 477 pp.) A remarkable and meticulous account of Meher Baba's *mast* tours and his work with the mad, the poor, and advanced seekers from 1922 to 1949. Features a preface by Baba about madness as opposed to enlightenment and includes comments about Baba by advanced aspirants.

Duce, Ivy Oneita. *How a Master Works.* Walnut Creek, Calif.: Sufism Reoriented, 1975. (Hardcover, 768 pp.) Distributed by Dodd, Mead & Co. An extraordinarily rich and valuable book highlighting the work of Meher Baba with his lovers. The text contains powerful lessons for Baba lovers; the Supplement is a gold mine of quotations and explanations.

Hopkinson, Tom, and Hopkinson, Dorothy. *Much Silence: Meher Baba—His Life and Work.* New York: Dodd, Mead & Co., 1975; London: Victor Gollancz, 1974. (Hardcover, 191 pp.) A fine, readable biography of Meher Baba. Not as detailed as *The God-Man,* but the best introductory biography yet to appear.

Irani, Manija S. *Family Letters.* New York: Society for Avatar Meher Baba, 1969; North Myrtle Beach, S.C.: Sheriar Press, 1976. (Softcover, 365 pp.) A series of personal letters written by Baba's sister-disciple to keep Westerners informed of the goings-on in India. A very rich source of Baba's activities, his work and suffering, plus direct quotes.

It So Happened: Stories from the Presence of Meher Baba. Edited by William LePage. Sydney: Meher Baba Foundation, forthcoming. (Softcover.) A collection of stories from Meher Baba's life, including stories about him, told to him, and used by him to illustrate spiritual discourses.

The Life Circulars of Avatar Meher Baba. Edited by Swami Satya Prakash Udaseen. Hyderabad, India: Meher Vihar Trust, 1968.

(Softcover, 140 pp.) These circulars were used by Meher Baba to describe his activities and issue instructions to followers worldwide. This collection covers the period mid-1952 to 1968.

Natu, Bal. *Glimpses of the God-Man, Meher Baba.* Walnut Creek, Calif.: Sufism Reoriented, forthcoming. Expanded from the diary of an Indian Baba lover now living at Meherazad. Tells of Bal Natu's experiences after meeting Baba and contains glimpses of Meher Baba's life and work between 1943 and 1948.

The New Life of Avatar Meher Baba and His Companions. Edited by Swami Satya Prakash Udaseen. Hyderabad, India: Meher Vihar Trust, 1967. (Hardcover, 314 pp.) A compilation of the "New Life Circulars," which form a journal of Baba's New Life, with stories and anecdotes of the unusual daily lives of the companions.

Nigam, Keshav Narayan. *Meher Chalisa.* Hamirpur, India: K. N. Nigam, 1962. (Hardcover, 99 pp.) Distributed by Meher Baba Information. Composed of forty photographs of Baba with an accompanying series of forty Hindi verses in praise of Baba, each translated into English.

Not We but One. Edited by William LePage. Sydney: Meher Baba Foundation, forthcoming. (Softcover.) Eleven chapters that feature Meher Baba's orientation on practical subjects such as childrearing, marriage, male-female roles, and everyday life. A large proportion of the book presents previously unpublished stories told by Eruch Jessawala and other disciples of Meher Baba.

Purdom, Charles B. *The God-Man.* North Myrtle Beach, S.C.: Sheriar Press, 1971. (Hardcover, 464 pp.) Detailed, well-documented description of phases of Meher Baba's life and work up through the early 1960s. Also includes verbatim discourses by Baba and conversations with his disciples and lovers. Although the author's final interpretation is his own and the book contains a few errors, it offers a wealth of information.

———. *God to Man and Man to God: The Discourses of Meher Baba.* North Myrtle Beach, S.C.: Sheriar Press, 1975. (Hardcover & softcover, 287 pp.) The author condenses the *Discourses* into a single, shorter version. Should not be considered as written by Baba because of the significant rewording of the original texts.

———. *The Perfect Master*. North Myrtle Beach, S.C.: Sheriar Press, 1976. (Softcover, 330 pp.) Originally published in 1937, this biography contains many details about Meher Baba's early life.

Schloss, Malcolm. *Ways to Attain the Supreme Reality by Shri Meher Baba, with Interpretations in Verse*. San Francisco: Sufism Reoriented, 1973. (Hardcover, 75 pp.) The book presents key messages of Baba given in the United States in 1952. The author illustrates them in verse, having been stimulated by a request from Baba to do so.

Shifrin, Adah, and Sargent, Patricia. *Meher Baba Is Love*. Miami, Fla.: Shifrin & Sargent, 1961. (Softcover, 56 pp.) Distributed by Sheriar Press. A delightful children's book of photos of Meher Baba with children and animals. Also includes verses illustrated in color.

Tales from the New Life with Meher Baba. Narrated by Eruch [Jessawala], Mehera [Irani], Mani [Irani], and Meheru [Irani]. Berkeley, Calif.: Beguine Library, 1976. (Softcover, 191 pp.) An account of Baba's New Life period, told primarily through interviews of mandali who traveled with Baba during that time.

Periodicals about Meher Baba

The Awakener. Edited by Filis Frederick. Hermosa Beach, Calif., Universal Spiritual League of America. Vol. 1 (1954) was quarterly; currently biannual. Distribution and subscription through P.O. Box 1081, Berkeley, Calif. 94701. A rich source over the years, this journal presents previously published and unpublished messages of Baba, personal accounts of disciples, and related material.

Divya Vani (Divine Voice). Visakhapatnam, India, Meher Nazar Publishing. Quarterly, 1962–1964; bimonthly, 1964–1965; monthly, 1965 to present. Subscriptions through Avatar Meher Baba Mission, 2–26–4, Sri Nagar, Kakinada–3, A. P., India. An erratic English-language monthly featuring occasional articles about Baba and Baba group activities in certain parts of India.

The Glow. Edited by Naosherwan Anzar. Dehra Dun, U.P., India, Glow Publications. Quarterly, 1966 to present. Distribution and subscriptions through F. Nalavala, 36, Lytton Road, Dehra Dun, U.P., India. English-language quarterly of growing quality. Articles about Baba, interviews with mandali, and photos highlight this magazine.

Meher Baba Journal. Ahmednagar, India, Elizabeth Patterson and the Meher Editorial Committee. Vols. 1–4, 1938–1942. Vol. 1 of the *Journal* has been reprinted recently by Sheriar Press. Edited by Western Baba lovers who were living in India, it features articles by and about Baba. Most significantly, Baba gave a discourse each month to the magazine that formed the basis of the published *Discourses.*

Meher Gazette. Bombay, Meher League. Vols. 1–7, 1930–1938. A small quarterly newspaper oriented to Baba, including poetry, prose, Baba's messages, and advertisements. Incorporated into the new *Meher Baba Journal* after 1938.

The Meher Message. Nasik, India, K. J. Dastur. Vols. 1–3, 1929–1931. The first regular periodical about Baba, issued in 1929. In it Baba gave some of his earliest and most esoteric discourses.

Other Publications of Interest

Brabazon, Francis. *The Word at World's End.* Berkeley, Calif.: John F. Kennedy University Press, 1971. (Softcover, 78 pp.) Distributed by Meher Baba Information. Hard-hitting narrative in a varied poetic style, this book delivers a devastating critique of current materialistic civilization viewed from a spiritual perspective.

Chapman, Rick. *How to Choose a Guru.* New York: Harper & Row, Perennial Library, 1973. (Softcover, 147 pp.) An easy-to-read, occasionally humorous rendering of important issues facing those seeking spiritual guidance. Based heavily on Meher Baba's orientation, it gives solid advice on a variety of practical topics.

Conybeare, Irene. *Civilization or Chaos.* 2d ed., rev. Bombay: Chetana, 1959. (Softcover, 251 pp.) A wide-ranging metaphysical treatise based on the teachings of Meher Baba, with reference to other Eastern and Western themes.

Duce, Ivy O. *What Am I Doing Here?* New York: Harper & Row,

Perennial Library, 1972. (Softcover, 111 pp.) Offers a readable introduction to a variety of spiritual themes based on Meher Baba's orientation. The author, a Sufi teacher, presents numerous illuminating anecdotes and perspectives on real as opposed to synthetic experience.

Harper, Marvin H. *Gurus, Swamis and Avataras: Spiritual Masters and Their American Disciples.* Philadelphia: Westminster Press, 1972. (Hardcover, 270 pp.) The author presents information on gurus and their followers, including chap. 4, "The Highest of the High," on Meher Baba, (pp. 54–77).

Nalavala, Naosherwan K. *In Lap of Love.* Dehra Dun, India: Chandna Printing Works, 1966. (Hardcover, 94 pp.) Statements of Meher Baba followed by the author's verse.

Needleman, Jacob. *The New Religions.* Garden City, N.Y.: Doubleday, 1970. (Hardcover & softcover, 245 pp.) An excellent examination of selected new American spiritual movements, including chap. 3, "Meher Baba," pp. 76–104.

Rowley, Peter. *New Gods in America.* New York: David McKay, 1971. (Hardcover, 208 pp.) A journalistically written survey of new spiritual groups, including chap. 14, "Meher Baba," pp. 120–134.

Sufism. Edited by Ivy O. Duce. San Francisco: Sufism Reoriented, 1971. (Softcover, 58 pp.) Articles on the nature of Sufism, the history of Sufism Reoriented, and the Sufi path.

A basic Meher Baba library might include the *Discourses; Listen, Humanity; Much Silence; The Everything and the Nothing; God Speaks;* and *Stay with God.* Also of introductory value are *What Am I Doing Here?* and *Avatar.*

There is not sufficient space to list all the books, pamphlets, and other publications written about Baba or inspired by him. Omitted here are the publications for children on Avataric and mystical themes, as well as new musical compositions dedicated to Baba. Also, there has been a gradual increase in foreign-language publications; along with translations in several Indian and Eastern languages, some Baba literature exists in French, German, Hebrew, and Spanish. Specialized publications are often listed by the major information centers, which also offer mail service for films, posters, record albums, tapes, and photographs.

APPENDIX D

Sources of Information about Meher Baba

Readers may wish to acquire more information on Meher Baba groups, locally available publications, local Baba lovers and so forth. As major sources of general and miscellaneous information about Meher Baba, the following information centers have carried on substantial communication by mail and have supplied booklists, whereabouts of local centers, and other Baba-related information:

The Meher Spiritual Center
P.O. Box 487
Myrtle Beach, South Carolina 29577
U.S.A.

Meher Baba Information
P.O. Box 1101
Berkeley, California 94701
U.S.A.

Sufism Reoriented, Inc.
1300 Boulevard Way
Walnut Creek, California 94595
U.S.A.

Meher Baba Association
Meher Baba Oceanic
The Boathouse, Ranleagh Drive
Twickenham TW1 1Q2
England

Meher House
12 Kalianna Crescent
Beacon Hill
New South Wales 2100
Australia

Avatar Meher Baba Trust
% Adi K. Irani
King's Road
Ahmednagar, Maharashtra
India

Meher Baba Groups and Centers

United States

Local Meher Baba centers in the United States also can be contacted for information. Some localities have a drop-in information center or bookstore; others have regular or informal Baba meetings. Naturally, local groups spring up constantly and change locations over the years. Usually, current addresses or contacts for local centers can be obtained through the U.S. information centers listed above. At the least, the following cities are likely to have active groups or centers:

Tucson, Phoenix (Arizona); Los Angeles, Berkeley–San Francisco, Santa Barbara (California); Denver–Boulder (Colorado); Miami, Tampa (Florida); Atlanta (Georgia); Honolulu (Hawaii); Chicago (Illinois); Baltimore (Maryland); Boston–Cambridge (Massachusetts); Detroit (Michigan); Minneapolis–St. Paul (Minnesota); northern New Jersey; New York City, Schenectady–Albany (New York); Chapel Hill (North Carolina); Portland (Oregon); Pittsburgh, Philadelphia (Pennsylvania); Myrtle Beach (South Carolina); Austin (Texas); Nashville (Tennessee); Hampton (Virginia); Seattle (Washington); Washington (D.C.).

Other Baba groups, meeting regularly or informally, exist in most states. Those interested in local contacts should write to the nearest information center. A current periodical of interest is the *Meher News Exchange East/West*, which gives news about Baba happenings in the West and in India. More information about the newsletter may be obtained from the Sheriar Press, P.O. Drawer 1519, North Myrtle Beach, South Carolina 29582, U.S.A.

Europe

England has generated the most formal Meher Baba activity in Europe. A major resource center is open to the public in the London suburbs. The English Baba lovers conduct regular meetings and offer a bookstore, as well as a film and audio tape library.

There are smaller groups also in Paris, Munich, and Vienna. Readers interested in European activity may contact the Meher Baba Association, Meher Baba Oceanic, The Boathouse, Ranleagh Drive, Twickenham, TW1 1Q2, England.

Asia

There are Meher Baba groups and centers in many towns and cities across India. There are a few active groups in Pakistan (for example, Karachi) and in Iran (for example, Teheran) and a small group in Jerusalem. The most stable source of information for the current locations of Asian centers is the Avatar Meher Baba Trust, % Adi K. Irani, King's Road, Ahmednagar, Maharashtra, India.

Australia–New Zealand

There are groups of Baba lovers in each capital city and other localities throughout Australia. Two centers are the most important. One is called Avatar's Abode, a name given by Meher Baba himself. It is near Woombye in Queensland. A close disciple of Meher Baba, Francis Brabazon, lives there permanently. There are sizable groups living around the area and meeting in the nearby city of Brisbane. Limited accommodation only is available for visitors to the property, but satisfactory arrangements can be made close by.

The second primary center is Meher House, located in the suburbs of Sydney. There is a large and active group in the area, with various meetings open to the public. Further information about Meher Baba activities in Australia may be obtained through Mr. William LePage, Meher House, 12 Kalianna Crescent, Beacon Hill, N.S.W. 2100, Australia.

In New Zealand, the relatively more modest activity by Baba lovers is increasing in many localities. Information about activity in any part of New Zealand will be provided by Mr. Anthony Thorpe, 3 Flowers Track, Christchurch 8, New Zealand.

Centers with Residential Facilities

There are two major centers of pilgrimage and retreat connected with Meher Baba. Each has a constant flow of visitors and maintains ample short-term residential facilities, although arrangements should be made in advance:

Ahmednagar area, India. Current home of the mandali, Baba's two ashrams, and his tomb. Local hotels and tourist homes. Write to: Adi K. Irani, King's Road, Ahmednagar, Maharashtra, India.

Myrtle Beach, South Carolina, U.S.A. A spiritual center and retreat on the ocean, visited by Baba in 1952, 1956, and 1958. Well-furnished cabins and kitchens. Write to: Meher Spiritual Center, P.O. Box 487, Myrtle Beach, South Carolina 29577, U.S.A.

Notes

Chapter 1, The Life of Meher Baba

1. Quoted in Charles B. Purdom, *The God-Man* (North Myrtle Beach, S.C., 1971), p. 244.
2. Quoted in Tom Hopkinson and Dorothy Hopkinson, *Much Silence: Meher Baba—His Life and Work* (New York, 1975), p. 25.
3. Meher Baba, *Listen, Humanity*, ed. Don E. Stevens (New York, 1971), p. 245.
4. Jean Adriel, *Avatar: The Life Story of the Perfect Master Meher Baba* (Berkeley, Calif., 1971), p. 44.
5. *Listen, Humanity*, p. 245.
6. Quoted in Purdom, *The God-Man*, p. 244.
7. *Listen, Humanity*, p. 247.
8. Quoted in Purdom, *The God-Man*, p. 244.
9. *Listen, Humanity*, pp. 248–249.
10. Ibid., pp. 249–250.
11. Ibid., p. 250.
12. Ibid., p. 253.
13. Ibid.
14. The Meher Ashram is movingly described in A. K. (Ramjoo) Abdullah, *Sobs and Throbs, or Some Spiritual Highlights* (Phoenix, 1969).
15. Adriel, *Avatar*, p. 166.
16. Quoted in Hopkinson and Hopkinson, *Much Silence*, p. 75.
17. *Listen, Humanity*, p. 260.
18. Ibid.
19. Adriel, *Avatar*, p. 216. Material on the New Life is found also in *The New Life of Meher Baba and His Companions*, ed. Swami Satya Prakash Udaseen (Hyderabad, India, 1967), and in *Tales from the New Life with Meher Baba*, narrated by Eruch [Jessawala], Mehera [Irani], Mani [Irani], and Meheru [Irani], (Berkeley, Calif., 1976).

20. D. E. Stevens, quoted in *Listen, Humanity*, p. 261.
21. Quoted in Purdom, *The God-Man*, p. 204.
22. Quoted in Manija S. Irani, *Family Letters* (New York, 1969), no. 78, p. 2.
23. Quoted ibid.
24. Hopkinson and Hopkinson, *Much Silence*, pp. 16–17.
25. Adriel, *Avatar*, p. 178.
26. *Listen, Humanity*, p. 126.
27. Quoted in Adriel, *Avatar*, p. 59.
28. *Listen, Humanity*, pp. 65–66.
29. Meher Baba, *Life at Its Best*, ed. Ivy O. Duce (New York, 1972), pp. 94–97.

Chapter 2, The Quest of Consciousness

1. *Listen, Humanity*, p. 151.
2. Meher Baba, *Discourses*, 3 vols. (San Francisco, 1967), 2 : 13–15.
3. Ibid., pp. 18–19.
4. *Listen, Humanity*, p. 152.
5. Meher Baba's definitive work on this subject is *God Speaks*, 2nd ed. (New York, 1973). A simpler introduction is given in Ivy O. Duce, *What Am I Doing Here?* (New York, 1972).
6. *Discourses*, 2 : 139.
7. Quoted in Francis Brabazon, *Stay with God* (Sydney, 1959), p. 107.
8. *Discourses*, 2 : 144–145.
9. Meher Baba, *The Everything and the Nothing* (Berkeley, Calif., 1971), p. 78.
10. Meher Baba, *Sparks from Meher Baba* (Myrtle Beach, S.C., 1962), pp. 9–10.
11. Ibid., p. 13.
12. *The Awakener*, vol. 10, no. 1 (1964), p. 29.
13. *Discourses*, 2 : 41.
14. Ibid., 1 : 20–21.
15. Ibid., 2 : 12.
16. Ibid., p. 191.
17. *Divya Vani*, vol. l, no. 11 (1966), p. 10 (hereafter the monthly series is assumed unless otherwise indicated).

Introduction to Part II

1. *Listen, Humanity*, p. 166.
2. *Discourses*, 1 : 65.
3. Ibid., pp. 62–64.

4. Ibid., pp. 66–67.
5. Ibid., 2 : 60.
6. Ibid., p. 67.
7. Ibid., p. 61.
8. *Life at Its Best*, pp. 35–36.
9. *Discourses*, 2 : 66.
10. Quoted in Purdom, *The God-Man*, p. 328.
11. Quoted in Brabazon, *Stay with God*, p. 13.
12. *Listen, Humanity*, p. 159.

Chapter 3, The Path of Knowledge

1. *Discourses*, 2 : 187.
2. Ibid.
3. Ibid., p. 189.
4. *Listen, Humanity*, pp. 160–161.
5. *Discourses*, 2 : 187–188.
6. *Listen, Humanity*, p. 159.
7. *Discourses*, 2 : 113–114, 116.
8. Ibid., pp. 112, 118.
9. Ibid., p. 121.
10. Ibid., pp. 124–125.
11. Quoted in C. D. Deshmukh, *My Master and His Teaching* (Ahmednagar, India, 1936), p. 13.
12. *The Awakener*, vol. 10, no. 2 (1964), pp. 15–16.
13. Ibid., vol. 3, no. 4 (1956), p. 31.

Chapter 4, The Path of Love

1. *Discourses*, 1 : 156–157.
2. Ibid., pp. 157–159, 161.
3. Ibid., pp. 159–160.
4. Ibid., 3 : 81.
5. Ibid., 1 : 146–147.
6. Ibid., p. 144.
7. Quoted in *The Answer: Conversations with Meher Baba*, ed. Naosherwan Anzar (Bombay, 1972), p. 2.
8. *Discourses*, 1 : 145.
9. Ibid., pp. 145, 149–150.
10. Ibid., p. 155.
11. Ibid., 3 : 180.
12. Ibid., 1 : 84.
13. Ibid., 2 : 69.

14. Ibid., 1 : 86.
15. Quoted in Francis Brabazon, *Journey with God and Messages of Meher Baba* (North Myrtle Beach, S.C., 1971), p. 35.
16. *The Awakener*, vol. 2, no. 3 (1955), p. 58.
17. Meher Baba, *Meher Baba on Love* (Poona, India, Meher Era Publications, 1970), p. 74.
18. *The Awakener*, vol. 5, no. 3 (1958), p. 53.
19. *Meher Baba on Love*, p. 74.
20. *Sparks*, p. 17.
21. Meher Baba, *Meher Baba's Universal Message* (Myrtle Beach, S.C., 1964).
22. *Discourses*, 1 : 24.
23. *Discourses*, 1 : 84.
24. Meher Baba, Precise citation misplaced.

Chapter 5, The Path of Action

1. *Discourses*, 2 : 189–190.
2. Quoted in *The Answer*, p. 34.
3. *God Speaks*, pp. 207–208.
4. *Meher Baba Journal*, vol. 1, no. 6 (1939), pp. 63–64.
5. *Listen, Humanity*, pp. 42–43.
6. *The Awakener*, vol. 3, no. 3 (1956), p. 12.
7. *Sparks*, p. 20.
8. *Discourses*, 1 : 72–73.
9. *Meher Baba Journal*, vol. 2, no. 2 (1939), p. 98.
10. *Divya Vani*, vol. 2, no. 1 (1962), pp. 13–14.
11. *Discourses*, 1 : 78–79.
12. Ibid., pp. 70–71.
13. Quoted in Ruth White, *Wisdom of Meher Baba* (Charleston, S.C., 1957), p. 56.
14. *Meher Baba Journal*, vol. 1, no. 2 (1938), p. 35.
15. *Discourses*, 2 : 68.
16. *Life at Its Best*, pp. 28–29.
17. *Meher Baba Journal*, vol. 1, no. 4 (1939), p. 93.
18. *The Awakener*, vol. 3, no. 1 (1955), p. 18.
19. Ibid., vol. 10, no. 2 (1964), p. 36.
20. *Life at Its Best*, p. 30.
21. *Sparks*, p. 18.
22. *Life at Its Best*, pp. 29–30.
23. *Listen, Humanity*, p. 159.
24. *Discourses*, 1 : 83.
25. Ibid., p. 31.

26. Ibid., p. 83.
27. Ibid., 3 : 126–127.
28. *The Awakener*, vol. 1, no. 3 (1954), p. 36.
29. *Divya Vani*, vol. 1, no. 11 (1966), p. 13.
30. *Discourses*, 3 : 126.
31. *Listen, Humanity*, p. 148.
32. Quoted in Adriel, *Avatar*, p. 264.
33. *Sparks*, p. 12.

Chapter 6, Spiritual Sidetracks

1. *Discourses*, 2 : 84.
2. Ibid., p. 87.
3. *The Awakener*, vol. 10, no. 1 (1964), p. 34.
4. Ibid., p. 5.
5. Quoted in Purdom, *The God-Man*, p. 245.
6. Quoted in *The Answer*, p. 26.
7. Meher Baba, *God in a Pill? Meher Baba on L.S.D. and the High Roads* (San Francisco, 1966), p. 6.
8. Ibid., p. 2.
9. Conversation with Robert Dreyfuss, Fall 1967.
10. *God in a Pill?*, pp. 5–6.
11. Meher Baba, *Beams from Meher Baba on the Spiritual Panorama* (New York, 1971), pp. 45–46.
12. *God Speaks*, p. 72.
13. *Beams from Meher Baba*, p. 46.
14. Quoted in A. K. Abdullah, *Sobs and Throbs*.
15. *Discourses*, 2 : 98–99.
16. See *God Speaks*, pp. 229–232.
17. *Meher Baba Journal*, vol. 2, no. 1 (1939), p. 91.
18. Precise citation misplaced; similar passage in *The Awakener*, vol. 3, no. 4 (1956), p. 15.
19. *The Awakener*, vol. 11, no. 2 (1966), p. 44.
20. Personal communication, Fall 1971.
21. Quoted in Irani, *Family Letters*, no. 55, p. 5.
22. *The Awakener*, vol. 5, no. 3 (1958), p. 26.
23. *Beams from Meher Baba*, pp. 68–69.
24. Purdom, *The God-Man*, p. 36.

Chapter 7, The Way of the Master

1. *Discourses*, 3 : 30–31.
2. Ibid., p. 34.

3. Ibid., p. 27.
4. Ibid., 1 : 88.
5. Ibid., p. 91.
6. Ibid., 2 : 73–74.
7. *Life at Its Best*, p. 18.
8. *Discourses*, 2 : 51.
9. Ibid., 3 : 39–40.
10. Ibid., 2 : 74.
11. Meher Baba, quoted in Charles B. Purdom, *The Perfect Master* (North Myrtle Beach, S.C., 1975), page citations misplaced.
12. *Discourses*, 2 : 81–82.
13. Ibid., pp. 179–180.
14. Quoted in Purdom, *The God-Man*, p. 37.
15. Irani, *Family Letters*, no. 77, p. 7.
16. Meher Baba, Precise quotation misplaced, probably from an unpublished collection of interviews with Baba, editor unknown.
17. Of interest in this regard is Rick Chapman's *How to Choose a Guru* (New York, 1973).
18. *Listen, Humanity*, pp. 163–164.

Chapter 8, Meher Baba: Avatar and Guide

1. *Listen, Humanity*, p. 227.
2. *Discourses*, 3 : 14–15.
3. Ibid., p. 14.
4. Baba has indicated that the Avatar appears in human form every 600 to 1,400 years, depending on the length of the historical cycle.
5. *Listen, Humanity*, pp. 227–228.
6. *Discourses*, 3 : 15.
7. Baba stated that John the Baptist played the same role for Jesus: **John the Baptist was a wonderful being. He gave his neck; he was the Master of Jesus** (quoted in Purdom, *The God-Man*, p. 255).
8. *The Awakener*, vol. 2, no. 3 (1955), p. 35.
9. Quoted in Irani, *Family Letters*, no. 51, p. 4.
10. *The Everything and the Nothing*, p. 77.
11. *The Awakener*, vol. 11, no. 1 (1966), p. 33.
12. Ibid., vol. 4, no. 2 (1957), p. 23.
13. Quoted in *The Answer*, p. 40.
14. *The Everything and the Nothing*, p. 72.
15. Ibid., p. 56.
16. Ibid., p. 77.
17. Quoted in Purdom, *The God-Man*, p. 369.
18. *The Awakener*, vol. 10, no. 1 (1964), p. 19.

19. Quoted in Purdom, *The God-Man*, p. 316.
20. Quoted ibid., p. 260.
21. *The Awakener*, vol. 1, no. 3 (1954), p. 12.
22. *Listen, Humanity*, p. 224.
23. *Sparks*, p. 6.
24. Quoted in *The Answer*, pp. 22–24.
25. Quoted in A.C.S. Chari, *An Introductory Sketch on the Life and Work of Avatar Meher Baba* (Calcutta, 1966), p. 23.
26. Quoted in Purdom, *The God-Man*, p. 256.
27. *God Speaks*, p. xxxvi.
28. Quoted in Purdom, *The God-Man*, pp. 343–344.
29. *Divya Vani*, vol. 1, no. 11 (1966), p. 15.
30. *Listen, Humanity*, p. xvii.
31. Quoted in Irani, *Family Letters*, no. 70, p. 6.
32. Quoted in Chari, *An Introductory Sketch*, pp. 22–23.
33. *The Awakener*, vol. 4, no. 3 (1957), p. 17.
34. Quoted in Purdom, *The God-Man*, p. 344.
35. Quoted ibid., p. 356.
36. Quoted in Irani, *Family Letters*, no. 53, p. 3.
37. *The Awakener*, vol. 2, no. 3 (1955), p. 81.
38. Quoted in Irani, *Family Letters*, no. 52, p. 2.
39. Quoted in Purdom, *The God-Man*, p. 392.
40. Quoted ibid., p. 260.
41. *Listen, Humanity*, p. 224.
42. Ibid.
43. *Divya Vani*, vol. 1, no. 8 (1966), p. 42.
44. *Listen, Humanity*, p. 227.
45. Quoted in Adriel, *Avatar*, p. 127.
46. Quoted in Purdom, *The God-Man*, p. 77.
47. Quoted in *The Answer*, p. 57.
48. Quoted ibid., p. 21.
49. Quoted in Irani, *Family Letters*, no. 47, p. 2.
50. Quoted in Purdom, *The God-Man*, p. 261.
51. *The Awakener*, vol. 9, no. 4 (1964), pp. 15–16.
52. *Discourses*, 1 : 138.
53. Quoted in Adriel, *Avatar*, pp. 97–98.
54. Quoted in Purdom, *The God-Man*, p. 254.
55. *Listen, Humanity*, p. 83.
56. Quoted in Purdom, *The God-Man*, p. 254.
57. Meher Baba, *Meher Baba's Call* (Ahmednagar, India, 1954), p. 1.
58. Meher Baba, *Six Messages* (Ahmednagar, date unknown).
59. *The Meher Message*, vol. 2, no. 2 (1930), p. 1.
60. *Sparks*, pp. 12–13.

61. Precise quotation misplaced.
62. *Discourses*, 3 : 16–17.

Chapter 9, Approaching the Avatar

1. *Divya Vani* (quarterly), vol. 1, no. 2 (1961), p. 32.
2. *Listen, Humanity*, pp. 13–14.
3. *The Awakener*, vol. 5, no. 4 (1958), p. 33.
4. Ibid., vol. 3, no. 3 (1956), p. 13.
5. Quoted in Purdom, *The God-Man*, p. 304.
6. *The Awakener*, vol. 8, no. 2 (1962), p. 6.
7. Quoted in Purdom, *The God-Man*, p. 319.
8. Quoted ibid., p. 135.
9. *The Awakener*, vol. 4, no. 1 (1956), p. 17.
10. Ibid., no. 2 (1957), p. 22.
11. Quoted in Purdom, *The God-Man*, p. 284.
12. Precise quotation misplaced.
13. *The Awakener*, vol. 8, no. 2 (1962), p. 6.
14. Meher Baba, *What Baba Means by Real Work* (Myrtle Beach, S.C., Universal Spiritual League, 1970), p. 6.
15. *Listen, Humanity*, p. 237.
16. Ibid., p. 20.
17. Ibid.
18. Meher Baba, *Darshan Hours* (Berkeley, Calif., 1973), p. 45.
19. *The Awakener*, vol. 9, nos. 1–2, (1963), p. 13.
20. Ibid., vol. 4, no. 2 (1957), p. 31.
21. *What Baba Means by Real Work* (Myrtle Beach, S.C., 1970), p. 6.
22. Quoted in Adriel, *Avatar*, p. 199.
23. *The Awakener*, vol. 9, nos. 1–2 (1963), p. 60.
24. Ibid., vol. 3, no. 1 (1955), p. 26.
25. Ibid., no. 2 (1955), p. 11.
26. Quoted in Irani, *Family Letters*, no. 13, p. 1.
27. *The Everything and the Nothing*, p. 42.
28. *Listen, Humanity*, p. 23.
29. Ibid.
30. *The Awakener*, vol. 3, no. 1 (1955), p. 26.
31. Quoted in Purdom, *The God-Man*, p. 72.
32. Sarosh Irani, transcript of interview, May 1972.
33. *Listen, Humanity*, p. 17.
34. Ibid., p. 163.
35. Quoted in Purdom, *The God-Man*, p. 230.

36. Dr. C. D. Deshmukh, *Meher Baba the Awakener* (published in India, details unknown).
37. Quoted in Brabazon, *Journey with God*, p. 34.
38. *The Awakener*, vol. 1, no. 3 (1954), p. 3.
39. Ibid., vol. 4, no. 4 (1957), p. 18.
40. *Divya Vani* (bimonthly), vol. 1, no. 3 (1964), p. 40.
41. *Sparks*, p. 7.
42. Precise citation misplaced; probably in *The Awakener*.
43. Quoted in Purdom, *The God-Man*, pp. 213–214.
44. *Listen, Humanity*, p. 17.
45. *Divya Vani* (bimonthly), vol. 1, no. 2 (1964), p. 1.
46. *The Everything and the Nothing*, p. 64.
47. *The Awakener*, vol. 3, no. 2 (1955), pp. 20–21.
48. *Divya Vani* (quarterly), vol. 3, no. 1 (1930), p. 48.
49. *Listen, Humanity*, p. 87.
50. Quoted in Purdom, *The God-Man*, p. 366.
51. *The Awakener*, vol. 9, no. 4 (1964), p. 16.
52. Quoted in Irani, *Family Letters*, no. 62, p. 5.
53. Quoted ibid., no. 80, p. 8.
54. Quoted in Purdom, *The God-Man*, p. 286.
55. *The Awakener*, vol. 4, no. 3 (1957), p. 41.
56. *Discourses*, 3 : 181–182.
57. *Listen, Humanity*, p. 190.

Chapter 10, Following the Way of Meher Baba

1. *Discourses*, 2 : 42–43.
2. *Beams from Meher Baba*, pp. 95–96.
3. *Listen, Humanity*, p. 176.
4. *The Awakener*, vol. 9, no. 4 (1964), p. 10.
5. *Beams from Meher Baba*, pp. 97–98.
6. *The Awakener*, vol. 4, no. 2 (1957), p. 14.
7. *Beams from Meher Baba*, pp. 98–100.
8. Purdom, *The God-Man*, p. 69.
9. *Life at Its Best*, pp. 59–60.
10. *Meher Baba Journal*, vol. 1, no. 3 (1939), p. 66.
11. Ibid., no. 6 (1939), p. 62.
12. *Discourses*, 3 : 133.
13. *Sparks*, p. 11.
14. *Discourses*, 3 : 132.
15. Ibid., pp. 132–133.
16. Ibid., p. 132.
17. Ibid., p. 133.

18. Ibid., p. 134.
19. Quoted in Purdom, *The God-Man*, p. 218.
20. Quoted in Adriel, *Avatar*, p. 137.
21. *The Awakener*, vol. 5, no. 4 (1958), p. 27.
22. *Divya Vani*, vol. 2, no. 1 (1939), p. 5.
23. *The Awakener*, vol. 11, no. 2 (1966), p. 44.
24. Ibid., vol. 1, no. 4 (1954), p. 5.
25. Adi K. Irani, in *Divya Vani*, vol. 5, no. 1 (1969), p. 8.
26. *Discourses*, 3 : 118–119.
27. Quoted in Purdom, *The God-Man*, p. 37.
28. *Discourses*, 3 : 119–121.
29. Quoted in Purdom, *The God-Man*, p. 48.
30. Quoted in *The Answer*, p. 11.
31. *Discourses*, 3 : 121.
32. *Meher Gazette*, vol. 2, no. 2 (1933), p. 1.
33. *The Awakener*, vol. 6, no. 4 (1960), p. 30.
34. Quoted in *The Answer*, p. 13.
35. *The Awakener*, vol. 4, no. 1 (1956), p. 16.
36. *Meher Baba Journal*, vol. 1, no. 9 (1939), p. 32.
37. *The Awakener*, vol. 11, no. 2 (1966), p. 44.
38. *Meher Baba Journal*, vol. 2, no. 9 (1940), p. 563.
39. *Discourses*, 3 : 169.
40. *Sparks*, p. 19.
41. *The Awakener*, vol. 3, no. 3 (1956), p. 13.
42. *Discourses*, 3 : 173.
43. *The Awakener*, vol. 3, no. 1 (1955), p. 18.
44. Ibid., vol. 1, no. 4 (1954), pp. 5–6.
45. Ibid., vol. 8, no. 4 (1962), p. 9.
46. Quoted in Adriel, *Avatar*, p. 230.
47. Precise citation misplaced; one rendering of the partial quotation is found in *The Awakener*, vol. 5, no. 3 (1958), pp. 39–40.

Chapter 11, Remembrance

1. *The Awakener*, vol. 6, no. 3 (1959), p. 25.
2. *Life at Its Best*, p. 19.
3. *Discourses*, 2 : 149.
4. *Sparks*, p. 8.
5. *The Everything and the Nothing*, p. 39.
6. *Listen, Humanity*, p. 44.
7. Quoted in Adriel, *Avatar*, pp. 255–256.
8. *The Awakener*, vol. 3, no. 1 (1955), p. 26.
9. Ibid., p. 20.

10. *God Speaks*, p. 208.
11. *The Awakener*, vol. 9, nos. 1–2, (1963), pp. 15–16.
12. *Listen, Humanity*, pp. 44–45.
13. *The Everything and the Nothing*, p. 62.
14. *The Awakener*, vol. 3, no. 3 (1956), p. 19.
15. *Discourses*, 2 : 95.
16. *The Awakener*, vol. 10, no. 2 (1964), p. 15.
17. Ibid., vol. 4, no. 2 (1957), pp. 30–31.
18. *Discourses*, 2 : 96–97.
19. *Listen, Humanity*, p. 45.
20. Quoted in Irani, *Family Letters*, no. 71, p. 6.
21. Quoted ibid., no. 41, p. 3.
22. Quoted in Brabazon, *Journey with God* (North Myrtle Beach, S.C., 1976), p. 34.
23. *Meher Baba Journal*, vol. 2, no. 9 (1940), p. 538.
24. Brabazon, *Stay with God*, pp. 111–112, 96.
25. *The Holy Qur-an*, trans. Abdullah Yusuf Ali (Washington, D.C., 1946), p. 1634.
26. *Meher Baba Journal*, vol. 1, no. 2 (1938), p. 30.
27. Meher Baba, *Sayings of Shri Meher Baba* (London, Circle Editorial Committee, 1933), p. 11.
28. Quoted in Purdom, *The Perfect Master*, p. 112.
29. *Divya Vani* (quarterly), vol. 1, no. 4 (1962), p. 56.
30. Quoted in Irani, *Family Letters*, no. 36, p. 2.
31. Quoted ibid., no. 34, p. 4.
32. *Divya Vani* (quarterly), vol. 3, no. 1 (1963), p. 12.
33. Quoted in Purdom, *The God-Man*, p. 320. This does not apply to suicide, which is discussed in *Listen, Humanity*, pp. 99–101.
34. Ibid., p. 337.
35. *The Bhagavad-Gita*, trans. Mohini Chatterji (New York, 1960), pp. 137–138.
36. Quoted in Purdom, *The God-Man*, p. 320.
37. Brabazon, *Stay with God*, p. 144.
38. *The Awakener*, vol. 3, no. 3 (1956), p. 13.
39. *Listen, Humanity*, p. 45.
40. *The Awakener*, vol. 8, no. 2 (1962), pp. 8–9.

Chapter 12, Doorways to the Mastery of Consciousness

1. Rano Gayley, transcribed interview, May 1972. One of the women mandali, Rano Gayley had been with Baba for over thirty years at the time of the interview. A talented American artist, she is the sole remaining Western mandali at Meherazad. (The Britisher Dr.

William Donkin dropped his body soon after Baba did, and Francis Brabazon moved back to his native Australia.)

2. Ali Akbar Shapurzaman, transcribed interview, May 1972. "Aloba" is the name Baba gave him, another of the mandali. Of Persian Muslim extraction, Aloba first met Baba in 1926, was in direct contact with him for almost twenty years, and was then called to live permanently with Baba in 1952.
3. Arnavaz Dadachanji, transcribed interview, October 1975. Arnavaz Dadachanji and her husband Nariman have been devoted Baba lovers for decades. They were assigned a worldly life by Baba, and Nariman became a successful industrialist and chemical engineer in Bombay. However, Baba drew them back to stay at Meherazad. Nariman dropped his body in 1974.
4. Adi K. Irani, Sr., transcribed interview, May 1972. A companion of Baba's for over forty-five years, Adi K. Irani is well known to Western Baba lovers as Baba's secretary-disciple and eloquent interpreter, having been responsible for much of the written communication between Baba and his lovers. This intimate mandali has his office and residence in Ahmednagar.
5. Arnavaz Dadachanji, October 1975.
6. Nariman Dadachanji, May 1972.
7. Ali Akbar Shapurzaman, May 1972.
8. Eruch Jessawala, transcribed interview, May 1972. Eruch Jessawala lived and journeyed with Meher Baba for decades. Increasingly, he was assigned as Baba's personal attendant and the primary interpreter of Baba's gestures. Baba called him "my right hand." Although Mr. Jessawala requested extensive editing or paraphrasing of his transcribed comments, most of his words are preserved relatively intact.
9. Manija Sheriar Irani, transcribed interview, May 1972. "Mani" is the younger sister of Merwan Irani (Baba). She was devoted to her elder brother as her Master while still a girl and was with Baba constantly at his ashrams as an intimate mandali as well as a major communication link to Western Baba lovers.
10. K. S. Sarosh Irani, transcribed interview, May 1972. Sarosh Irani left his physical body eight months after this interview. He was with Baba for forty-five years, having been instructed to live the worldly life in nearby Ahmednagar. A beloved husband and father, he was deeply respected by the townspeople, who elected him mayor and supported several of his successful businesses. The Indian army appointed him an honorary lieutenant colonel. His dedication to Baba was total.
11. Meherjee Karkaria, transcribed interview, May 1972. Meherjee Karkaria first met Baba in 1927 and has been under Baba's direction

and instructions for decades. A family man who spent many years in Iran, he followed Baba's orders to pursue business and eventually built a very successful manufacturing concern in Poona. Baba often called for him, and he has long been considered one of the close mandali.

12. Manija Irani, May 1972.
13. Adi K. Irani, transcribed interview, October 1975.
14. Ibid.
15. Bhau Kulchuri, transcribed interview, October 1975. Bhau is one of the youngest of the male mandali. Besides being a faithful companion of Baba's for many years, Bhau was instructed by Baba to write a titanic biography constructed entirely in Hindi verse.
16. Adi K. Irani, May 1975.
17. Sarosh Irani, May 1972.
18. Eruch Jessawala, May 1972.
19. Adi K. Irani, October 1975.
20. Erich Jessawala, October 1975.
21. Ibid.
22. Arnavaz Dadachanji, October 1975.
23. *The Everything and the Nothing*, p. 19.
24. Ibid., p. 50.

Chapter 13, Reactions to Meher Baba

1. *Life at Its Best*, p. 58.
2. Ibid., pp. xiii–xiv.
3. Dr. W. Y. Evans-Wentz, in a descriptive brochure about *God Speaks*.
4. *Daily Express* (London), April 10, 1932; quoted in Adriel, *Avatar*, p. 136.
5. Irene Conybeare, *In Quest of Truth, or How I Came to Meher Baba* (Kakinada, India, circa 1960), p. 250.
6. Chari, *Introductory Sketch*, p. 20.
7. D. E. Stevens, quoted in *God Speaks*, p. xv.
8. D. E. Stevens, in *Listen, Humanity*, p. 226.
9. Adriel, *Avatar*, p. 135.
10. Ibid., p. 14.
11. Ibid., pp. 281–283.
12. Brabazon, *Journey with God*, pp. 3–4.
13. Ibid., p. 17.
14. Purdom, *The God-Man*, p. 85.
15. Ibid., p. 95.
16. William Donkin, *The Wayfarers* (San Francisco, 1969), pp. 151, 153–156.

17. Irani, *Family Letters*, no. 7, p. 2.
18. Newspaper accounts of this event were widespread in the Eastern world, including *The Bombay News*, February 17, 1969; the Karachi newspaper *Jang*, February 7; and the Saudi Arabian paper *Al Nadwa*, some time in February 1969.
19. *Life at Its Best*, p. i.
20. Quoted in Adriel, *Avatar*, p. 138, and from a collection of interviews with Meher Baba.

Chapter 14, Final Declarations

1. Dr. H. P. Bharucha, *Meher Baba's Last Sahavas* (Navsari, India, H. P. Bharucha, 1969).
2. Irani, *Family Letters*, no. 81, p. 7.
3. Meher Baba, *Twenty-One Fragments* (Bombay, Meher Baba Centre, 1959), p. 18.
4. Quoted in Irani, *Family Letters*, no. 81, p. 1.
5. Quoted in Purdom, *The God-Man*, p. 272.
6. *Listen, Humanity*, p. 14.
7. Adi K. Irani, recorded interview, May 1972.
8. Adi K. Irani, in *Divya Vani*, vol. 5, no. 1 (1969), p. 5.
9. Eruch Jessawala, conversation in India, 1969, published in *How a Master Works*, by Ivy O. Duce, (Walnut Creek, Calif., 1975) p. 706.
10. Manija Irani, recorded interview, May 1972.
11. Quoted in Purdom, *The God-Man*, p. 278.
12. Quoted ibid.
13. Quoted ibid.
14. Quoted ibid., pp. 278–279.
15. Quoted ibid., p. 291.
16. Meher Baba, *Warning from Baba to His Lovers* (Ahmednagar, India, 1957).
17. *The Awakener*, vol. 8, no. 1 (1961), p. 3.
18. Ibid., vol. 3, no. 3 (1956), p. 8.
19. Ibid., vol. 4, no. 3 (1957), p. 16.
20. Ibid., vol. 3, no. 4 (1956), p. 14.
21. Quoted in Irani, *Family Letters*, no. 80, p. 3.
22. *The Awakener*, vol. 10, no. 3 (1965), p. 20.
23. Quoted in Purdom, *The God-Man*, p. 355.
24. Adi K. Irani, in "Baba Warns His Lovers," a letter circulated on July 10, 1968.
25. Manija Irani, in *The Awakener*, vol. 7, no. 2 (1960), p. 9.
26. *Darshan Hours*, p. 60.
27. Quoted in Irani, *Family Letters*, no. 52, p. 3.

28. *The Awakener*, vol. 5, no. 4 (1958), p. 27.
29. Meher Baba, in *Warning from Baba to His Lovers* (Ahmednagar, India, Adi K. Irani, 1957), p. 16.
30. Adi K. Irani, recorded interview, May 1972.
31. Eruch Jessawala, recorded interview, May 1972.
32. Eruch Jessawala, quoted in Hopkinson and Hopkinson, *Much Silence*, p. 45.

Chapter 15, The Meher Baba Movement

1. Adi K. Irani, in *Divya Vani*, vol. 6, no. 7 (1970), p. 44.
2. Hopkinson and Hopkinson, *Much Silence*, p. 42.
3. *Sparks*, pp. 14–15.
4. Quoted in Purdom, *The God-Man*, pp. 302–303.
5. *Listen, Humanity*, p. 71.
6. *Sufism*, ed. Ivy O. Duce (San Francisco, 1971).
7. Quoted in my "Meher Baba and Sufism Reoriented, Inc.," in *Sufism*, ed. Duce, p. 28.
8. Quoted ibid., p. 29.
9. Quoted ibid., pp. 29, 23.
10. Quoted in Hopkinson and Hopkinson, *Much Silence*, p. 57.
11. *Meher Baba's Call*, pp. 1, 4.